F4F WILDCAT
VS
A6M ZERO-SEN
Pacific Theater 1942

EDWARD M. YOUNG

First published in Great Britain in 2013 by Osprey Publishing, Midland House, West Way, Botley, Oxford OX2 0PH, UK

43-01 21st Street, Suite 220B, Long Island City, NY, 11101, USA

E-mail: info@ospreypublishing.com

A CIP catalog record for this book is available from the British Library.

ISBN: 978 1 78096 322 8
PDF e-book ISBN: 978 1 78096 323 5
e-Pub ISBN: 978 1 78096 324 2

Edited by Tony Holmes
Cover artworks and battlescene by Gareth Hector (www.garethhector.co.uk/aviation-art/)
Three-views, cockpits, gunsight and armament scrap views by Jim Laurier
Index by Michael Forder
Originated by PDQ Digital Media Solutions, UK
Printed in China through Asia Pacific Offset Limited

13 14 15 16 17   10 9 8 7 6 5 4 3 2 1

Osprey Publishing is supporting the Woodland Trust, the UK's leading woodland conservation charity, by funding the dedication of trees.

www.ospreypublishing.com

Acknowledgments

I would like to express my deep gratitude to my good friend Osamu Tagaya for generously sharing his exceptional knowledge of Imperial Japanese Navy Air Force (IJNAF) aviation. Over many years Sam has been a source of astute observations and insights on IJN fighters and fighter tactics. His comments and suggestions for this *Duel* volume were invaluable. I am indebted to Linda Cheek-Hall and Elizabeth Cheek-Jones for allowing me to use photos of their father, then-Machinist Tom Cheek of VF-3, and to quote from a memoir he wrote on his experiences at Midway. Ms Sarah Serizawa translated several Japanese sources that provided insight into the great affection Zero-sen pilots had for their aircraft, and their experiences fighting against the Wildcat. The photographs in the volume came from the Australian War Memorial, the Still Pictures Branch at the National Archives and Records Administration, the National Museum of Naval Aviation and the Museum of Flight. I would like to thank the staffs of these organizations and particularly Amy Heidrick at the Museum of Flight. Ben Kristy at the National Museum of the Marine Corps and Dr James Ginther at the Marine Corps' History Division kindly responded to inquiries on the transmission of fighter tactics. Lastly, I would like to acknowledge an intellectual debt to John Lundstrom and Mark Peattie. In the preparation of this volume I have relied heavily on John Lundstrom's excellent studies of US Navy fighter combat during 1942, *The First Team – Pacific Naval Air Combat from Pearl Harbor to Midway* and *The First Team and the Guadalcanal Campaign – Naval Fighter Combat from August to November 1942*, and Mark Peattie's equally excellent *Sunburst – The Rise of Japanese Naval Air Power, 1909–1941*. These works are highly recommended for those who want to pursue the duels between the Wildcat and the Zero-sen in more detail.

F4F Wildcat cover art

Between October 18 and 25, 1942, Capt Joseph Foss, Executive Officer of VMF-121, claimed 13 Zero-sens shot down over Guadalcanal. Although relatively new to flying fighters, Foss had more than 1,000 hours of flying time when he went into combat. He benefited from having studied the manual on fighter tactics written by Lt Cdr James "Jimmy" Flatley when he took command of VF-10, this volume incorporating Flatley's experiences fighting the Zero-sen during the Battle of the Coral Sea. Foss developed a healthy respect for the Zero-sen's maneuverability. Writing in his autobiography years later he said, "At the time, it was the best fighter in the world. It could beat our Wildcats in interception, maneuverability, climb and speed. A Zero could turn on a dime and climb like a scared monkey on a rope." But the Zero-sen was vulnerable to enemy fire, quickly exploding when hit by rounds from the Wildcat's six 0.50in. machine guns. Foss learned to get in close to a Zero-sen before opening fire. "Because I usually shot from very close range," Foss wrote, "the Zeros almost always exploded, which was quite a sight. There was a bright flash when the gas tanks blew, and the engine would spin off by itself in a lopsided whirl. When a Zero blew up in front of you there was nowhere to go except right through the pieces." (Cover artwork by Gareth Hector)

A6M Zero-sen cover art

Late on the morning of May 8, 1942, two sections of F4F-3 Wildcats from VF-2, flying off USS *Lexington* (CV-2), were escorting VT-2's TBD Devastators on their way to attack the Japanese carriers *Shōkaku* and *Zuikaku* when four patrolling Type 0 fighters from the latter aircraft carrier jumped them. Catching the Wildcats as they flew slowly along with their charges, the Zero-sen pilots used slashing hit-and-run attacks to quickly shoot down the two wingmen, Ens Dale Peterson and Ens Richard Rowell. Forced to fight for his life, division leader Lt Noel Gaylor managed to evade the Zero-sen attacks long enough to find safety in a nearby cloud formation. Exiting the clouds, Gaylor found a Zero-sen and fired at it, claiming a probable. The returning VF-2 pilots reported that the enemy fighters had resorted to "violent maneuvering, consisting of loops, rolls, and steeply banked turns," and confirmed that they seemed to be armed with 20mm cannon and two rifle-caliber machine guns. Although three Wildcats failed to return from the mission, the After Action Report noted that "present leak-proof tanks were very effective for preventing fires and loss of gasoline when tanks were punctured. Armor is effective against glancing blows by 20mm cannon and from direct blows by small-caliber shells." The Wildcat's rugged construction and protection for fuel tanks and pilot would give it a decided advantage over the more fragile and less well-protected Zero-sen in the air battles that followed. (Cover artwork by Gareth Hector)

CONTENTS

Introduction   4

Chronology   8

Design and Development   10

Technical Specifications   25

The Strategic Situation   35

The Combatants   41

Combat   49

Statistics and Analysis   73

Aftermath   77

Further Reading   79

Index   80

INTRODUCTION

Rarely in the annals of air combat has a fighter airplane made such a sudden and dramatic impact as the Mitsubishi Zero-sen in the first few months of the Pacific War. Arriving seemingly out of nowhere, the Type 0 Carrier Fighter (A6M2 Reisen, or Zero-sen in English) of the Imperial Japanese Navy Air Force (IJNAF) swept all before it as the armed forces of Imperial Japan rampaged through Southeast Asia and the Pacific. To the astonishment of their pilots, the fighter airplanes of the American, British and Dutch air and naval forces – Curtiss P-40s and Hawk 75s, Brewster Buffaloes and Hawker Hurricanes – were roughly handled and pushed aside in the overwhelming tide of Japanese conquest.

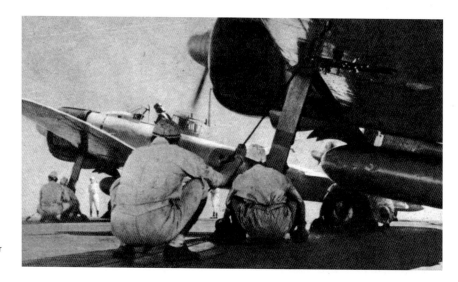

Crewmen wait for the signal to remove the chocks from Type 0 Model 21s on the deck of a carrier in early 1942. (via the author)

The Zero-sen fighters of the IJNAF's carrier- and land-based kokutai (air group) rapidly established air superiority wherever they encountered Allied fighters, appearing to be almost invincible. Fast, well armed, highly maneuverable, with exceptional range and climbing ability, and flown by skilled and experienced pilots, the Zero-sen's appearance and performance came as a distinct shock. Indeed, its dominance during the first year of the Pacific War would become legendary. Over time the Zero-sen would become as iconic an airplane for the Japanese as the Spitfire was for the British.

The extent of the West's rude awakening was due in no small measure to the disparity between the Western view of Japan and Japanese technological abilities, and the Zero-sen's superlative performance. Prior to the outbreak of the war, Western views of Japan's aviation industry were dismissive and wrapped in racial stereotypes. It was widely believed that Japanese airplanes were decidedly inferior to their western counterparts, as were Japanese aircrews. Few observers gave the Japanese any credit for originality or independent invention.

An article in the March 1941 edition of British aviation magazine *The Aeroplane* stated that, "The Japanese are, by nature, imitators and lack originality. Japanese aviation has, therefore, a long way to go before it will be able to compete successfully with, or even combat, the 'decadent European and American democracies'." An American aviation writer commented in a similar vein that the Japanese "have not yet gotten much beyond merely imitating what others have done. At that they are the World's finest, but imitativeness is little help in aeronautics." And yet, in its March 1939 Information Bulletin on the conflict then raging in China, the US Navy's Office of Intelligence had warned against this very complacency. "No possible benefits can be derived," the report read, "from underestimating their war-making powers on the land, on the sea or in the air." Yet the western powers badly underestimated Japan's capabilities, to their cost.

An F4F-4 Wildcat taxis in after returning from a mission over Guadalcanal in late 1942. The stalwart F4F was the principal fighter of the US Navy and the US Marine Corps throughout the first year of the Pacific War. (127GR-3-50898, Record Group 127, National Archives and Records Service (NARA))

The Japanese surprise attack on Pearl Harbor on December 7, 1941 made it inevitable that there would be battles between the aircraft carrier forces of the IJNAF and the US Navy. This was a battle that both sides had expected, planned for and trained for. In the carrier battles that took place during 1942, the premier carrier fighters of the two navies, the Japanese Type 0 Carrier Fighter and the US Navy's Grumman F4F Wildcat, came into confrontation. This confrontation continued as land-based Zero-sen units and US Marine Corps and Navy Wildcats joined in furious air battles over Guadalcanal.

The duel between the Zero-sen and the Wildcat is a classic example of the challenge a pilot faces when dealing with an adversary flying a more capable aircraft. The Zero-sen was, in many respects, superior to the Wildcat. The Japanese fighter had a better rate-of-climb, was faster and was far more maneuverable. It could out-climb, out-turn and be on the tail of a Wildcat in a heartbeat. The encounters between the Zero-sen and the Wildcat at the battles of the Coral Sea and Midway demonstrated the Japanese fighter's superiority in no uncertain terms.

The US Navy and Marine Corps pilots flying the Wildcat during 1942 had to develop tactics that exploited the few advantages (more rugged construction and superior armament) the Grumman fighter had over the Zero-sen, while negating the Mitsubishi's advantage in maneuverability. Fortunately for America, these tactics did emerge in time. Building on the lessons Lt Cdr James Flatley distilled from his experiences during the Battle of the Coral Sea, US Navy and Marine Corps Wildcat pilots learned to adopt hit-and-run attacks against the Zero-sen. They also avoided low-speed maneuvering combat, where the Japanese fighter excelled. Finally, US Navy and Marine Corps pilots took advantage of the Zero-sen's greatest weaknesses – its lack of protection for fuel and pilot, which meant that the airplane was unable to absorb damage.

The last sight that many an Allied pilot glimpsed in his rear-vision mirror prior to being shot down during the early months of the Pacific War. This particular Zero-sen is a clipped-wing A6M3 Model 32. (via Aerospace Publishing)

Lt Cdr John "Jimmy" Thach developed a defensive weaving maneuver that enabled two pilots or two sections to provide mutual support to each other when under attack. Successfully tested at Midway, this maneuver came to be called the "Thach Weave" and remained in use against the Zero-sen throughout the war. This combination of defensive and offensive tactics enabled US Navy and Marine Corps Wildcat pilots to inflict heavy losses on the IJNAF's Zero-sen units during the grueling battle of attrition over Guadalcanal.

When the IJNAF attacked Pearl Harbor the United States was not prepared for war. The US Congress had passed the Two-Ocean Navy Act in July 1940, approving the construction of 18 new aircraft carriers and authorizing 15,000 aircraft for the US Navy and the Marine Corps, but it would take time for the carriers and airplanes to be built and to train the men to man them. Newer and more powerful fighter airplanes were under development – the Vought XF4U Corsair and the Grumman XF6F, for example – but these, too, were by no means ready when America was attacked. The US Navy and the Marine Corps went to war with the Grumman F4F Wildcat, the best carrier fighter available at the time.

Naval Aviators flying the Wildcat, and their compatriots in the US Army Air Forces, had to hold the line against the Japanese onslaught until America's vast industrial capacity could produce the newer and better weapons needed to defeat Japan. Knowing that it faced a much stronger enemy, Japan's strategy was to fight America to exhaustion and hopefully inflict a decisive defeat as quickly as possible. Grumman's Wildcat fighter helped derail the Japanese plan.

Bronzed and gaunt Marine TSgt R. W. Greenwood was plane captain for this F4F-4 Wildcat on Guadalcanal. Flown by multiple pilots, the airplane miraculously survived to claim 19 victories over Japanese aircraft. (208-AA, Box 115, Folder E-1, RG 208, NARA)

CHRONOLOGY

1935
August The US Navy's Bureau of Aeronautics initiates a design competition for a new carrier fighter.

1936
March US Navy awards the Grumman Aircraft Company a contract for one XF4F-1 biplane fighter.

July US Navy places a contract for a completely revised Grumman design as the XF4F-2 monoplane fighter.

1937
May IJN issues preliminary planning document for the Prototype 12-shi Carrier-based fighter, intended as a replacement for the A5M Type 96 Carrier Fighter.

July Beginning of the Sino-Japanese Incident.

September A5M Type 96 Carrier Fighter makes its combat debut over China.

September 2 First flight of the Grumman XF4F-2.

October IJN issues its final Planning Requirement for the Prototype 12-shi Carrier Fighter.

1938
June After trials of both the XF4F-2 and the XF2A-1, the US Navy places an order for 54 Brewster F2A-1 carrier fighters, rather than the Grumman design.

October US Navy awards Grumman a contract for the improved XF4F-3 fighter.

1939
February 12 XF4F-3 makes its first flight.

April 1 Mitsubishi Prototype 12-shi Carrier Fighter makes its first flight.

August US Navy awards Grumman a contract for 54 F4F-3 fighters.

Groundcrew from a land-based fighter Kokutai wave off a pilot of a Zero Model 21 in early 1942. (via the author)

An F4F-3 from VF-6 prepares to take off from USS *Enterprise* (CV-6) in early 1942. Note the 100lb bomb beneath the fighter's starboard wing. (80G-14540, RG 80, NARA)

1940

February	First flight of the production F4F-3.
July	Yokosuka Kokutai sends the Type 0 fighter to China for operational testing.
September 13	Zero-sen pilots claim 27 Chinese fighters shot down over Chungking.
December	Deliveries of the F4F-3 commence, with VF-4 and VF-7 receiving the first examples.

1941

April 14	XF4F-4 makes its first flight.
December 7	Attack on Pearl Harbor.

1942

May 7–8	Battle of the Coral Sea.
June 4	Battle of Midway.
August 7	Intensive air battles commence over Guadalcanal, lasting three months.
August 20	VMF-223 lands on Guadalcanal with 19 F4F-4s.
August 24–25	Battle of the Eastern Solomons.
October 26	Battle of Santa Cruz.

1943

February	VMF-124 arrives on Guadalcanal with the first Vought F4U-1 Corsairs.

This early model A6M3 was abandoned by the Tainan Kokutai at Buna, New Guinea, in late 1942 after suffering battle damage. (via Aerospace Publishing)

DESIGN AND DEVELOPMENT

F4F WILDCAT

In the mid-1930s, the US Navy began the transition from the biplane to the monoplane. The streamlined, all-metal, stressed skin monoplane with enclosed cockpit, flaps and retractable landing gear, with engines of increasing horsepower, pointed to a future where performance would considerably surpass the biplane.

During 1934, the US Navy's Bureau of Aeronautics awarded contracts for prototypes of a new all-metal monoplane torpedo-bomber, the Douglas XTBD-1, and for new monoplane dive-bombers, with contracts for the Brewster XSBA-1, Northrop XBT-1 and Vought XSB2U-1. A year later, in August 1935, the Bureau sent out a request for a competitive design of a new single-seat fighter. The Bureau informed the manufacturers that it wanted to continue development of high-performance fighters, and requested that the designs submitted have the maximum performance possible. This meant a top speed exceeding 250mph within restrictions of size and weight, and a stalling speed of not more than 65mph. The Bureau appears not to have specified a preference for a monoplane or a biplane, and stated that folding wings were "not necessary or desirable."

The request for higher maximum speeds reflected the Bureau's concern at the time that the speed margin between the latest monoplane bombers and biplane fighters was declining. The US Navy's then-current fighters, the Curtiss BF2C-1 and the

Grumman F2F-1, had a less than 20mph speed advantage over the US Army Air Corps' Martin B-10 bomber, and the newer Grumman F3F-1, ordered that summer, was no better. That same August the Seversky SEV-1, precursor of the Seversky P-35, achieved a top speed of 284mph in tests for the USAAC at Wright Field – well in excess of the BF2C and the F3F. Hedging its bets after reviewing preliminary design submissions, the Bureau of Aeronautics purchased an experimental monoplane from the Brewster Aeronautical Corporation and a more conservative biplane from the Grumman Aircraft Corporation in November 1935.

Founded in 1929 by Leroy Grumman, the Grumman Aircraft Corporation had won a contract in 1931 for its first US Navy carrier fighter, the two-seat FF-1 biplane. The single-seat F2F-1 followed in 1934, the portly fighter replacing the older Boeing F4B aboard US Navy carriers and establishing Grumman as the leading manufacturer of American carrier fighters. Flight tests on the similar but improved Grumman F3F-1 had begun during 1935, providing a starting point for the US Navy's design request issued in August. On March 2, 1936, Grumman was awarded a contract for its proposal, the XF4F-1. The company had submitted a design for a biplane fighter – basically a refinement of its F3F-1, but with a more powerful 800hp Pratt & Whitney or Wright engine, giving an estimated top speed of 264mph. The aircraft was armed with single 0.30in. and 0.50in. machine guns in the nose.

Two developments soon made the success of this proposal doubtful. Grumman's engineers had calculated that equipping its F3F-1 with the 950hp Wright XR-1820 Cyclone engine would push its top speed to over 255mph – close to the estimate for the XF4F-1. Then in June 1936 the US Navy awarded a contract to Brewster for the XF2A-1 monoplane fighter. Grumman duly abandoned the XF4F-1, with the US Navy's concurrence, and submitted a completely new design for a monoplane

A Grumman F3F-3 from VF-5. Grumman engineers found that when fitted with the more powerful 950hp Wright XR-1820 Cyclone radial engine, the F3F-3's top speed would be close to that of the biplane XF4F-1 – its intended replacement! (72-AC-18D-3, RG 72, NARA)

The revised Grumman XF4F-2. With the US Navy's concurrence, Grumman abandoned the biplane XF4F-1 design for a revised monoplane fighter. The XF4F-2 had an armament of two 0.50in. machine guns in the nose, with the provision for two more in the wings. (72-AC-18E-7, RG 72, NARA)

fighter designated the XF4F-2. Following a review of detailed design drawings, wind tunnel tests on a scale model and inspection of a mock-up, Grumman received a contract on July 28, 1936 for this new airplane.

The XF4F-2 retained the XF4F-1's retractable landing gear and cockpit location, the latter giving the pilot good visibility over the nose for both landing and gunnery. Grumman placed the new monoplane wing at mid-fuselage. The US Navy wanted the newly developed Pratt & Whitney XR-1830-66 engine fitted in one of its experimental fighters, so Grumman obliged accordingly. The XR-1830 was a 14-cylinder, two-row engine with single-stage supercharger, offering 1,050hp on takeoff and 900hp at 9,000ft, with the possibility of even more power with further development. Grumman engineers estimated that this engine would give the XF4F-2 a top speed of 290mph.

Interestingly, in light of its future battles with the cannon-armed Mitsubishi A6M Type 0 Carrier Fighter, the US Navy requested the capability of mounting two 20mm cannon in the wings of the XF4F-2 in addition to two 0.50in. machine guns in the nose, synchronized to fire through the propeller. However, the initial armament fitted to the prototype consisted of only the two 0.50in. machine guns in the nose, with the provision for two more 0.50in. weapons mounted in the wings. At the insistence of frontline units in the Fleet, which at the time wanted fighters that were also capable of dive-bombing, the XF4F-2 featured mountings for two 100lb bombs under the wings.

The XF4F-2 made its first flight on September 2, 1937 at Grumman's plant at Bethpage, Long Island. It was subsequently sent to Naval Air Station (NAS) Anacostia, on the outskirts of Washington, D.C., where the fighter commenced official US Navy trials alongside the Brewster XF2A-1 and the Seversky NF-1 (a navalized equivalent to the USAAC's P-35). The testing program lasted into April 1938 and included a thorough evaluation of the flight characteristics and armament of each of the three airplanes.

Problems with the Pratt & Whitney engine hampered testing of the XF4F-2, causing one serious accident when the engine cut out shortly after takeoff from the Naval Aircraft Factory in Philadelphia, where the airplane had been conducting catapult tests and simulated carrier landings. Despite having a higher speed than the XF2A-1, the US Navy decided in June 1938 to place a contract with Brewster for 54 production versions of the XF2A-1.

The US Navy, however, was sufficiently impressed with the potential of Grumman's entry to continue its development. In October 1938 Grumman received a contract for a revised XF4F-3. The new fighter incorporated the heavier, but more powerful Pratt & Whitney XR-1830-76 engine, with a two-stage, two-speed supercharger providing 1,200hp for takeoff, 1,050hp at 11,000ft and 1,000hp at 19,000ft.

The XF4F-2 also had a provision to install fittings that allowed a 100lb bomb to be carried under each wing in place of the wing-mounted 0.50in. machine gun. Grumman retained the portly fuselage and retractable landing gear from the XF4F-1 design. (72-AC-18E-17, RG 72, NARA)

The XF4F-2 in flight. Problems with the Pratt & Whitney XR-1830-66 engine hampered the test flights, but the Grumman design proved sufficiently promising to encourage the US Navy to continue with its development. (80G-2824, RG 80, NARA)

The revised XF4F-3 featured a more powerful Pratt & Whitney R-1830-76 engine and squared-off wings and horizontal and vertical stabilizers. (80G-2826, RG 80, NARA)

After extensive flight tests, including time spent in the NACA wind tunnel at Langley, Virginia, the XF4F-3 was modified to improve its aerodynamic stability. The area of the vertical tail was increased, the horizontal stabilizers raised and a turtledeck section fitted between the cockpit and the vertical tail. (80G-2882, RG 80, NARA)

Grumman increased the wingspan from 34ft to 38ft and added square tips to the wing, the horizontal tailplanes and the vertical tail. The larger wing brought the XF4F-3's wing loading with the heavier engine back to within acceptable limits.

The XF4F-3 made its first flight on February 12, 1939 and then began six months of intensive flight tests at Bethpage and Anacostia. With the newer engine and supercharger, the XF4F-3 achieved a maximum speed of 333.5mph during the US Navy tests. In July, the US Navy's Bureau of Inspection and Survey, which had completed flight tests on the XF4F-3, recommended that the Grumman fighter be accepted as a service type, despite a conclusion that the fighter was longitudinally and laterally inadequate in landing. Accordingly, the following month, after nearly two years of effort, the US Navy awarded Grumman a contract for 54 F4F-3 fighters.

In late 1939 the XF4F-3 went to the National Advisory Committee for Aeronautics' full-scale wind tunnel at Langley, Virginia, where tests led to several aerodynamic refinements to improve the stability issues. The area of the vertical tail was increased and moved slightly back, increasing the length of the XF4F-3 by 19 inches, while

the tailplanes were raised 20 inches to the base of the tail fin. An extended turtledeck was also added between the tail fin and the cockpit, giving a smoother contour.

The first production F4F-3 made its maiden flight during February 1940. The first two aircraft had an armament of two 0.30in. machine guns in the nose and a single 0.50in. machine gun in each wing, but all subsequent F4F-3s had the nose-mounted weapons removed in favor of two additional 0.50in. machine guns in each wing. Armor plating was also fitted, but at this time the F4F-3 did not have self-sealing fuel tanks.

The first deliveries of production F4F-3s were not to the US Navy but to the Royal Navy's Fleet Air Arm, which had taken over a French order for 100 Wright Cyclone-powered aircraft after the fall of France in June 1940. Placed into service as the Martlet I, these airplanes achieved the Grumman fighter's first aerial victory when a Luftwaffe Ju 88 bomber was shot down on Christmas Day 1940. The first production F4F-3 for the US Navy, BuNo 1845, arrived at Anacostia on August 20, 1940. Deliveries to frontline squadrons began during December 1940 when VF-4, assigned to the air group embarked in USS *Ranger* (CV-4), and VF-7, aboard USS *Wasp* (CV-7), received their first airplanes.

The F4F soon demonstrated a clear superiority over the F2A, becoming the US Navy's choice for its fighter squadrons. Following the fall of France, the US Congress approved a substantial increase in appropriations for US Navy aircraft carriers and airplanes through the Two-Ocean Navy Act. Grumman received production orders for more F4Fs, ending the year with contracts covering the construction of 578 examples.

Concerned with persistent difficulties with the R-1830-76's two-stage supercharger, the US Navy had an F4F-3 fitted with a single-stage, two-speed supercharged Pratt & Whitney R-1830-90 engine in the fall of 1940. Although the re-engined fighter

VF-4, assigned to USS *Ranger* (CV-4), was one of the first units to receive production F4F-3s in December 1940. The F4F-3 had an armament of two 0.50in. machine guns in each wing. Early versions retained the telescopic sight. (72-AC-19-4A, RG 72, NARA)

The F4F-4 began replacing the F4F-3 in early 1942, its folding wings enabling the US Navy to embark more airplanes aboard its fleet carriers. However, the added weight associated with the folding-wing mechanism, along with more armor protection and two additional 0.50in. machine guns in the wings, made the F4F-4 more sluggish and less maneuverable than the F4F-3. (72-AC-19G-8, RG 72, NARA)

OPPOSITE
During his time on Guadalcanal, VMF-223's Capt Marion Carl flew two Wildcats that bore the side number black "13". He scored 12 victories flying his first "13", BuNo 02100, depicted here. Remarkably, Carl was at the controls of this aircraft on September 9, 1942 when, on his 13th mission, a Zero-sen shot him down just after he had claimed his 13th victory! Bailing out at 22,000ft, Carl landed in the sea off Guadalcanal. A local native rescued Carl and brought him back to land. With the help of other natives, he made his way back to Henderson Field five days later, where he discovered that his squadronmates had given away his few belongings when he had been declared missing in action! Not one to be superstitious, Carl selected another F4F-4 and had it numbered "13" too. He scored his last two Wildcat victories (a Type 1 bomber and a Zero-sen) in this second "13", F4F-4 BuNo 03508.

(designated the XF4F-6) handled just the same, it now had a lower maximum speed of 319mph. As a precaution against delays with the two-stage supercharged engine, the US Navy ordered 95 R-1830-90-powered fighters, re-designated F4F-3As. Thirty were assigned to a Greek order, but they were diverted to the Fleet Air Arm as Martlet IIIs following the capture of Greece by Axis forces in the spring of 1941. The remaining 65 were allocated to US Navy and US Marine Corps fighter squadrons. As more F4F-3s and the F4F-3As became available during 1941, they went to US Navy and US Marine Corps fighter squadrons on both the east and west coasts. Some squadrons operated a mix of both aircraft.

On October 1, 1941 the US Navy announced that it was giving names to many of its warplanes. The Grumman F4F duly becoming the "Wildcat," the first in a long line of Grumman feline names. At the time of the attack on Pearl Harbor, eight US Navy squadrons (VF-3, VF-5, VF-6, VF-8, VF-41, VF-42, VF-71 and VF-72) and three US Marine Corps squadrons (VMF-111, VMF-121 and VMF-211) were equipped with the Wildcat, with Grumman having delivered 183 F4F-3s and 65 F4F-3As.

The Grumman-built Wildcat variant that saw the most combat service, the F4F-4, was developed following the US Navy's interest in acquiring a folding-wing version of the fighter so that it could embark more aircraft on a carrier. In March 1940 the company developed a folding-wing mechanism and installed it in an F4F-3. Legend has it that Grumman engineers worked out the concept using a rubber eraser and paper clips. The folding-wing section, attached to two stubs connected to the fuselage, allowed the outer wings to be pivoted back against the fuselage, thus reducing the span from 38ft to a little over 14ft. As the XF4F-4, the airplane made its first flight on April 14, 1941. At first the folding-wing mechanism was hydraulic, but to save weight the hydraulic system was removed and the wings folded manually. The US Navy added an additional 0.50in. machine gun in each of the XF4F-4's wings.

The first F4F-4s appear to have been assigned to VF-71 on board *Wasp* in February 1942, followed by VF-8 on board USS *Hornet* (CV-8), both carriers then serving with the Atlantic Fleet. By the end of May 1942, most of the US Navy's fighter squadrons, and two Marine Corps squadrons, had converted to the F4F-4. During the course of that year Grumman would deliver 1,164 F4F-4s to the US Navy and the US Marine Corps.

F4F-4 WILDCAT

28ft 9in.

11ft 1in.

38ft 0in.

A6M TYPE 0 CARRIER FIGHTER (ZERO-SEN)

On October 5, 1937, the IJN's Koku Hombu (Aviation Bureau) sent its "Planning Requirements for the Prototype 12-shi Carrier-based Fighter" to the Mitsubishi Kokuki K.K. (Mitsubishi Aircraft Company Ltd) and the Nakajima Hikoki K.K. (Nakajima Aeroplane Company Ltd.). This document listed the final design requirements for a fighter airplane to replace the Mitsubishi A5M Type 96 Carrier Fighter then on active service in China.

Five months earlier, the Koku Hombu had issued its preliminary requirement for a new carrier fighter, and had begun discussions with the two airplane companies. Jiro Horikoshi, who had designed the A5M, participated in these conferences, and in the following months started working on some ideas for a new fighter. His A5M had been a quantum leap over its predecessor, the Nakajima A4N1 biplane fighter. An all-metal, semi-monocoque low-wing monoplane fighter with fixed landing gear, the A5M was faster and had a longer range than the A4N1, but was still highly maneuverable. At the time of its entry into service, the A5M was the first monoplane carrier fighter in service in any navy, and was without a doubt the finest carrier fighter in the world. The IJNAF was now asking Mitsubishi and Nakajima to make another quantum leap in fighter design.

In the months between May and October 1937, the IJNAF had entered combat over China in what became known as the Sino-Japanese "Incident." As the Koku Hombu worked to refine its requirements for a new carrier fighter, the bureau benefited from combat reports coming in from units on the China front. Perhaps the most influential of these concerned heavy losses sustained by the IJNAF's Mitsubishi G3M Type 96 Attack Bombers during unescorted bombing missions. Entering combat in mid-September, the Type 96 Carrier Fighter and its skilled pilots quickly established air superiority over the Chinese fighters they encountered, allowing the bombers to attack targets with impunity.

The Mitsubishi Prototype 12-shi Carrier-based Fighter was intended to replace the Mitsubishi A5M Type 96 Carrier Fighter, two of which (from the 12th Kokutai) are seen here on patrol over China in 1939. Initially, IJNAF pilots were reluctant to transition from the well-liked A5M to the new Zero-sen, as in mock dogfights with the latter fighter the Type 96 won every time. However, the spectacular first combat success enjoyed by the A6M in September 1940 changed pilots' minds once and for all. (via Robert C. Mikesh)

Although enjoying great success over China when engaging enemy fighters, A5M pilots found it difficult to knock down Chinese bombers with the Type 96's two 7.7mm machine guns. Recommendations began coming in to the Koku Hombu calling for a fighter with greater range, heavier armament and even better performance in speed and altitude. These recommendations coincided with the IJNAF's own evolving view of the role of the carrier fighter from simple air defense over the fleet to acting as escort to a carrier strike force, clearing the skies of enemy fighters for the accompanying dive- and torpedo-bombers.

The requirements laid down in the planning document the Koku Hombu circulated in October called for an airplane with a performance equal to or better than any other fighter in the world. The IJNAF wanted a machine that had the range to escort its bombers all the way to their targets, with a combat performance superior to any enemy fighters it might encounter. But the IJNAF still needed a fighter that could defend the fleet against air attack with an armament powerful enough to defeat enemy bomber and attack aircraft. Specifically, the Planning Requirement called for the following;

- A maximum speed in excess of 310mph
- Ability to climb to 9,800ft in 3 minutes, 30 seconds
- A range of 1,010 miles with a normal fuel load and 1,685 miles with an auxiliary drop tank
- Maneuverability equal to or better than the A5M Type 96 Fighter
- A wingspan of no more than 39ft 4in. (12 meters)
- Armament of two 20mm cannon in the wings and two 7.7mm machine guns in the nose
- Ability to take off in less than 230ft into a 30mph wind (essentially from a carrier deck)
- A landing speed of less than 67mph

Jori Horikoshi immediately realized that the IJNAF's individual requirements were incompatible with each other. To meet the range requirement, an escort fighter would have to carry a considerable amount of fuel in addition to the weight of the 20mm cannon, implying the need for a large, heavy airplane with a large powerful engine, while an interceptor fighter needed to have an exceptional rate-of-climb and superlative maneuverability – performance only a lighter weight airplane could achieve. As a Japanese aeronautical engineer described the challenge some years later, the Imperial Japanese Navy was asking for the aeronautical equivalent of an athlete with the endurance of a marathon runner, the speed of a sprinter, the powerful punch of a heavyweight boxer and the quick footwork of a welterweight. The Nakajima Company soon bowed out, leaving Jiro Horikoshi and his design team with the unenviable task of trying to make the impossible possible.

Horikoshi lacked a suitable engine for his new design. The weight, power, shape, fuel consumption and dimensions of the engine determined the shape of the fuselage and how much drag it created, as well as the fighter's weight, wing area and probable performance.

Japanese aviation engine development lagged behind that of America and Europe, for in the 1930s Japan was still an industrializing nation. The machine tool and automotive industries – foundations for the production of aircraft engines – were small

The A6M Type 0 Carrier Fighter's large wing, low wing loading and long ailerons gave the Zero-sen exceptional maneuverability at low speeds, making carrier landings no more difficult than in the Type 96 fighter. (Author's collection)

OPPOSITE
This A6M2 Zero-sen Model 21 belonged to the 3rd Kokutai, one of the IJNAF's leading land-based fighter units. The fighter, along with 20 other A6M2s, had arrived at Rabaul on September 17, 1942 from the Netherlands East Indies. Ordered to reinforce the Tainan Kokutai, the 3rd was re-designated the 202nd Kokutai on November 1, 1942 and transferred back to the Netherlands East Indies shortly thereafter. During the fighting over Guadalcanal, this particular aircraft had been flown by two of the 3rd Kokutai's aces, namely hikōtaicho (flying unit leader) Lt Takahide Aioi, who had claimed four victories fighting in China in the Type 96 Carrier Fighter, and PO2/c Yoshiro Hashiguchi, another China veteran. Both men made several claims while based in Rabaul and were ultimately credited with around ten victories each. Hashiguchi was killed during the Pacific War, but Aioi survived to retire as an admiral in the post-war Japanese Maritime Self-Defense Force.

and comparatively less well developed. In its planning requirements the Koku Hombu had specified two engines for the new carrier fighter design, the Mitsubishi "Zuisei" (Holy Star) and the Mitsubishi "Kinsei" (Golden Star), both 14-cylinder, two-row radial engines. Horikoshi preferred the Kinsei-46 engine for his design, as its 1,070hp rating was superior to the Zuisei-13's rating of 870hp, but the Kinsei was heavier and had a larger diameter and higher fuel consumption than the Zuisei. This would have required a larger and heavier airframe to accommodate both the engine and more fuel. Using the Zuisei-13 instead, Horikoshi and his team calculated that they could build a fighter weighing around 5,000lb – some 1,600lb less than an airplane equipped with a Kinsei-46.

Therein lay the source of the Zero-sen's superlative performance, but also its inherent flaw – vulnerability to combat damage. To fulfill the IJNAF's exacting requirements with an engine of around 900hp, Horikoshi and his team had to design as light an airplane as possible, yet still make it strong enough to stand up to the rigors of carrier operations. It also had to be capable of carrying sufficient fuel and armament to allow the airplane to function effectively as a fighter.

Weight reduction became the priority for the new aircraft, prevailing over concerns about ease of manufacturing or maintenance. Breaking with the traditional approach to structural strength, Horikoshi realized that not every part in the airplane had to conform to the IJNAF's standard safety factor of 1.8 times the expected maximum load. Wherever possible, the design team used a safety factor slightly below the 1.8 standard. To eliminate the heavy fittings normally used to attach the wing to the fuselage, the wing was designed as a single element running from the root to the tip, integral with the fuselage center section.

Fortuitously, the Sumitomo Metal Company had just developed a new strong zinc-aluminum alloy, known as Extra Super Duralumin, which meant thinner sheets of ESD could be used for the fighter's skinning. Every single component of the new fighter was carefully evaluated for further weight reduction. Armament for the pilot and self-sealing fuel tanks were not considered due to weight restrictions, although the Zero-sen was not unique in this respect as few of the world's fighter aircraft incorporated these protections at the time. The result was an airplane that was light in weight for its size, but not flimsy. Examining captured Zero-sens later in the war, American engineers were impressed that its strength compared favorably to American airplanes.

A6M2 ZERO-SEN MODEL 21

28ft 8in.

X·101

10ft 0in.

39ft 4.7in.

To provide the necessary maneuverability, Horikoshi designed a relatively large wing with a low wing loading, although this reduced the fighter's diving and level speeds. The larger wing allowed for the installation of the 20mm cannon and extra fuel tanks for added range. Horikoshi added a slight downward twist of the wing at the tip to delay the onset of wingtip stall, thereby improving lateral control and maneuverability. Each wing was also fitted with a long aileron. The fighter's excellent lateral stability made it easier to land on carrier decks. IJNAF pilots were to find the Zero-sen no more difficult to land than the earlier Type 96 fighter.

To make the fighter a better gun platform, the design team lengthened the fuselage and increased the area of the vertical and horizontal tail. The use of flush riveting and careful attention to aerodynamic refinement reduced drag, thereby improving speed and range. A streamlined drop tank (one of the first employed on a fighter) helped boost the range to meet the IJNAF's requirement, while wide retractable landing gear facilitated carrier landings. The new fighter incorporated a fully enclosed cockpit, with a streamlined canopy providing excellent vision all around.

The first flight of the Prototype 12-shi Carrier Fighter took place on 1 April 1939 from the airfield at Kagamigahara, 30 miles from the Mitsubishi Aircraft Company factory in Nagoya. After making several ground runs to test the brakes, Mitsubishi's chief test pilot Kasuzo Shima took the airplane aloft on a short flight, traveling 1,500ft down the runway at 30ft before returning to report that all control surfaces operated effectively. The brakes fitted to the fighter were inadequate, however. With the first flight accomplished, Mitsubishi began an intensive flight program to test the new fighter's stability and control.

On May 1, 1939, the Koku Hombu advised Horikoshi that the IJNAF intended to replace the Mitsubishi Zuisei-13 engine with the Nakajima "Sakae" (Prosperity). The Sakae-12 was also a 14-cylinder radial engine offering 950hp, and it was only slightly larger in diameter than the Zuisei-13. First installed on the third prototype, the Sakae would power almost every model of the Zero-sen fighter until the final months of the war. At the same time the IJNAF designated the first and second prototypes of the 12-shi fighter the A6M1 and the Sakae-powered model the A6M2.

Lt Saburo Shindo, flying Type 0 Model 21 AI-102, starts his takeoff run along the deck of *Akagi* as part of the second-wave attack on Pearl Harbor. The Zero-sen's drop tank – one of the first to be regularly carried on a fighter – helped give the aircraft phenomenal range for a single-engined machine.

(via Aerospace Publishing)

After completing tests with Mitsubishi, the first prototype was turned over to the IJNAF in September 1939, the second prototype following a month later. Flight tests had confirmed that in most respects the A6M1 fighter had met the IJNAF's specifications except for maximum speed. With the change to the Sakae engine, the A6M2 achieved a maximum speed of 331mph, exceeding the initial requirement. By any measure this outstanding fighter was a remarkable achievement for Jiro Horikoshi and his design team.

On July 31, 1940, the IJNAF formally accepted the Mitsubishi A6M2 as the Type 0 Carrier Fighter Model 11 (shortened to Reisen, or Zero-sen Fighter, in Japanese). The Type 0 designation was based on the year of introduction into service – 2600 (1940 AD) – according to the Japanese Imperial calendar.

Even before formal acceptance, the IJNAF Navy sent a small batch of 15 Zero-sens to China for operational testing with the 12th Kokutai, based at Hankow. When the first examples arrived at the airfield, cheers went up among the pilots and groundcrews as these exciting new fighters landed. The Type 96 pilots were in awe of the Zero-sen at first, with its enclosed cockpit, retractable landing gear and the impression it gave of speed and power. The few experienced pilots chosen to fly the A6M soon found it to be exceptional, easily outperforming the Type 96 fighter.

The Zero-sen formation flew its first mission on August 19, 1940, but the airplane did not engage Chinese fighters in combat until September 13. Escorting Type 96 bombers to Chungking, the Zero-sen pilots returned to the city after the bombers had departed to find 30 Polikarpov I-15bis and I-16 fighters circling over the target area. In a ferocious ten-minute air battle the Japanese pilots claimed 27 Chinese fighters shot down.

By the end of 1940 pilots flying the Zero-sen had claimed 59 fighters shot down and an additional 101 destroyed on the ground, all for the loss of just three airplanes to anti-aircraft fire. The legend of the Zero-sen's invincibility originated with this performance in China.

To make the fighter an easier fit on the elevators of the IJN's aircraft carriers, Mitsubishi fitted folding wingtips beginning with the 65th production aircraft. This led to a change in designation, this and subsequent aircraft being designated the Type 0 Carrier Fighter Model 21. A more intractable problem was the emergence of aileron flutter, which caused the death of two pilots in accidents. The IJNAF had installed

A6M2 Type 0 Model 21 fighters running up on the deck of *Shokaku*, waiting for the carrier to turn into the wind so that they can take off for the attack on Pearl Harbor on December 7, 1941. (80G-71198, RG 80, NARA)

balancing tabs on the ailerons in an attempt to improve responsiveness at higher speeds, but this apparently contributed to the problem. Working intensively, Mitsubishi found a solution to the problem by thickening the outer wing skin, increasing the torsional strength of the wing and adding small external balances to it. Fortunately for the IJNAF, these fixes were in place before the start of the Pacific War.

The Zero-sen fighter demonstrated superlative performance at low to medium speeds and low to medium altitudes. The very elements that gave the airplane its superb low-speed maneuverability – its large wing with low wing loading and long ailerons – caused the Zero-sen to lose maneuverability as speeds increased. At speeds above 180mph aileron response became sluggish and at speeds above 230mph the controls stiffened considerably and aileron control became poor. While the Zero-sen had a high operational ceiling, engine power fell off at higher altitudes, and the airplane's light weight and thin skinning limited its diving speeds. Pilot reports from China recommended improving high-speed aileron control and altitude performance.

In mid-1941, Mitsubishi began testing a prototype of a new Zero-sen model, designated the A6M3, equipped with a more powerful Sakae 21 engine of 1,130hp. At the suggestion of test pilots, Mitsubishi eliminated the folding wing feature, shortening the wingspan by three feet, and installed blunt wingtips. This also reduced the length of the ailerons by about a foot, improving the rate of roll at higher speeds for a small loss in overall maneuverability. Although the gain in maximum speed was a disappointment (the A6M3 was only some 6-8 mph faster than the A6M2), the new model entered production in early 1942 as the Type 0 Carrier Fighter Model 32 to indicate both a change in engine and a change in overall configuration.

By the time the IJNAF went to war on December 7, 1941, the A6M had replaced the older A5M in almost all of its fighter units. During 1941 the Mitsubishi Aircraft Company delivered 409 Zero-sens to the IJNAF. In an ironic turn, given its earlier withdrawal from the competition, the Nakajima Aircraft Company was also ordered to begin production of the Type 0 Fighter – the firm delivered its first aircraft to the IJNAF in November 1941.

On the first day of the Pacific War, the six aircraft carriers of the 1st Kōkū Kantai (1st Air Fleet) had more than 100 A6M2 fighters on strength, while the land-based 11th Kōkū Kantai (11th Air Fleet) deployed around 120 A6M2s in the 21st, 22nd and 23rd Kōkū Sentais (Air Flotillas), principally in the 3rd and Tainan Kokutais. The several hundred Zero-sen pilots available had been through a rigorous selection process, resulting in them being both highly trained and supremely confident in their ability. They were also acutely aware of the quality of their Zero-sen fighters. Many began the war with combat experience in China. They were, in all likelihood, the finest group of carrier fighter pilots in any navy in 1941.

TECHNICAL
SPECIFICATIONS

F4F WILDCAT

XF4F-2

The XF4F-2 was an all-metal mid-wing monoplane with an Alclad stressed-skin covering over metal bulkheads and stringers. The wings featured a single main spar, with the outer panels attached to a center section bolted to the fuselage. Flaps beneath the wings were pneumatically operated. The XF4F-2 retained the barrel-shaped fuselage, enclosed cockpit and rounded wingtips, vertical and horizontal stabilizers of the earlier F2F and F3F fighters, but had a slightly wider span and longer fuselage. Ailerons, elevators and rudder were fabric covered.

The Grumman fighter featured what was for the time a heavy armament – two 0.50in. machine guns in the upper cowling of the fuselage and two more mounted in the wings. Alternatively, the wing guns could be replaced with mounts for a single 100lb bomb under each wing. Two Plexiglas windows were fitted into the fuselage beneath the wing to give some downward visibility. The landing gear was similar to the F2F/F3F, with main wheels retracting into the fuselage under the wings. The gear could be raised or lowered with 30 turns of a hand crank in the cockpit. The powerplant was the Pratt & Whitney XR-1830-66, a two-row, 14-cylinder air-cooled radial engine with a single-stage, single-speed supercharger giving 1,050hp for takeoff and 900hp at 12,000ft.

XF4F-3

The revised XF4F-3 featured an increase in wingspan from 34ft to 38ft and a lengthened fuselage, while retaining the overall shape of the XF4F-2. The wingtips, horizontal stabilizers and vertical fin and rudder took on the squared-off, rectangular form that became characteristic of Grumman's wartime aircraft. Flight and wind tunnel tests resulted in an increase in the area of the vertical fin, the addition of a dorsal fillet between the vertical fin and the top of the fuselage and a raised horizontal stabilizer.

Armament changed to two cowl-mounted 0.30in. machine guns and two 0.50in. weapons in the wings. A more powerful Pratt & Whitney XR-1830-76 engine with a two-stage, two-speed supercharger replaced the earlier XR-1830-66, giving 1,200hp on takeoff and 1,000hp at 19,000ft. With this engine the XF4F-3 attained a maximum speed of 334mph at 20,500ft, with a gross weight of 6,099lb.

F4F-3

The first production model of the F4F fighter, the first two examples built had the same armament as the XF4F-3, but all subsequent aircraft featured an armament of four 0.50in. machine guns in the wings with 430 rounds per gun. By the end of the 1930s the US Navy had realized that the 0.30in. weapon was outdated following the advent of all-metal aircraft and the introduction of armor and self-sealing fuel tanks. Fighters needed greater punch, so the US Navy abandoned the 0.30in. weapon in favor of a battery of 0.50in. machine guns. While the latter did not have the destructive power of the 20mm cannon, it did have a higher rate of fire and a higher muzzle velocity, giving longer range.

For a brief period F4F-3 Wildcats wore the colorful pre-war markings that identified individual aircraft carriers. This F4F-3 from VF-42, with a red tail indicating its assignment to USS *Yorktown* (CV-5) and yellow wings, taxis out behind another F4F-3 from VF-7 painted in the duller light gray Neutrality camouflage scheme. (Peter M. Bowers Collection, Museum of Flight)

Early production aircraft had a telescopic sight protruding through the front windscreen, but this was later replaced with a N2AN reflector gunsight as these became available. Like the XF4F-3, the production aircraft had non-folding wings. The F4F-3 was equipped with the Pratt & Whitney R-1830-76 engine or the similar R-1830-86. When the F4F-3s were delivered to US Navy and US Marine Corps squadrons they did not have self-sealing fuel tanks and featured only limited armor plate protection for the pilot.

The Wildcat was a rugged airplane, able to stand up to repeated carrier landings, which British Naval observers likened to "controlled crashes." Gross weight was normally 7,065lb. The F4F-3 had a service ceiling of 37,000ft and a nominal range of 860 miles. By the end of 1941, Grumman had delivered 185 F4F-3s to the US Navy and the US Marine Corps.

XF4F-6/F4F-3A

Concerned about nagging problems with the Pratt & Whitney R-1830-76 engine, and the potential delays these could cause in their delivery, the US Navy ordered Grumman to test one F4F-3 fitted with the Pratt & Whitney R-1830-90 engine, with a single-stage, two-speed supercharger. Designated the XF4F-6, its flying characteristics were essentially the same as the F4F-3, but the XF4F-6 proved to be around 10mph slower at altitude. The US Navy gave Grumman a contract for 95 of these aircraft, re-designated F4F-3As. The Greek government was allocated 30 aircraft from this contract, and these machines found their way to the Fleet Air Arm as Martlet IIs following Greece's capture by German and Italian forces. The remaining 65 served with US Navy and US Marine Corps squadrons.

The F4F-3A was virtually indistinguishable from the F4F-3, the main difference being a different Pratt & Whitney engine. Many of the F4F-3As went to US Marine Corps fighter squadrons, as shown here. This machine is camouflaged in the light gray Neutrality scheme. (RG 208-AA-Box 115-Folder E-4, NARA)

The great advantage of the F4F-4 Wildcat was its folding wings, which meant that US Navy fleet carriers could carry more fighters. This in turn allowed fighter squadrons to boost their complement of Wildcats from 18 to 36 aircraft. Two F4F-4s could fit on the elevator of an aircraft carrier that could previously take only one F4F-3. (80G-16961, RG 80, NARA)

F4F-4

The F4F-4 was a major redesign of the F4F-3 to accommodate folding wings and greater armament. The F4F-4 was the main Wildcat model to see combat during 1942, with Grumman completing production of 1,169 aircraft by the end of the year. These were all allocated to US Navy and US Marine Corps fighter squadrons.

The adoption of a folding wing, reducing the span of the Wildcat from 38ft to 14ft on a carrier flightdeck, proved invaluable when the need to equip vessels with more fighter aircraft became evident following the battles of the Coral Sea and Midway.

The F4F-4 featured an additional 0.50in. machine gun outboard of the two wing guns, with 240 rounds per gun. While increasing the Wildcat's firepower, this change resulted in a reduction in the total amount of ammunition carried – a retrograde step in the view of many pilots, who after experiencing combat with Japanese aircraft thought that the four 0.50in. machine guns of the F4F-3 were perfectly adequate for dealing with the less-ruggedly constructed Zero-sen.

Reports from combat in Europe and the first few months of the war in the Pacific saw the hurried addition of self-sealing fuel tanks and around 150lb of armor for the oil tank and behind the pilot's seat, with a 27lb bullet-resistant windscreen replacing the earlier standard glass windshield. All the additions added around 900lb to the Wildcat's gross weight, with no increase in engine power. As a result, maximum speed dropped from 331mph in the F4F-3 to 318mph in the F4F-4 and rate-of-climb from 2,300ft per minute to 2,190ft per minute. The heavier F4F-4 was also less maneuverable than the F4F-3 – another retrograde step in the eyes of many Wildcat pilots.

F4F-4 WILDCAT MACHINE GUNS

The F4F-4 model of the Wildcat featured three Browning M-2 0.50in. machine guns in each wing (one more than in the preceding F4F-3), with the third gun placed outboard of the inner two weapons. The M-2 had a rate of fire of 750–850 rounds per minute, which meant that a two-second burst from all six machine guns sent about 80 rounds towards a Zero-sen. Adding the two extra machine guns forced a reduction in rounds per weapon from 450 rounds in the F4F-3 to 240 rounds in the F4F-4 – a retrograde step in the eyes of many pilots, who thought four 0.50in. machine guns adequate against the vulnerable Zero-sen, and preferred having more ammunition available. Some, like Capt Joe Foss, used only four of their six machine guns in an effort to make their ammunition last longer.

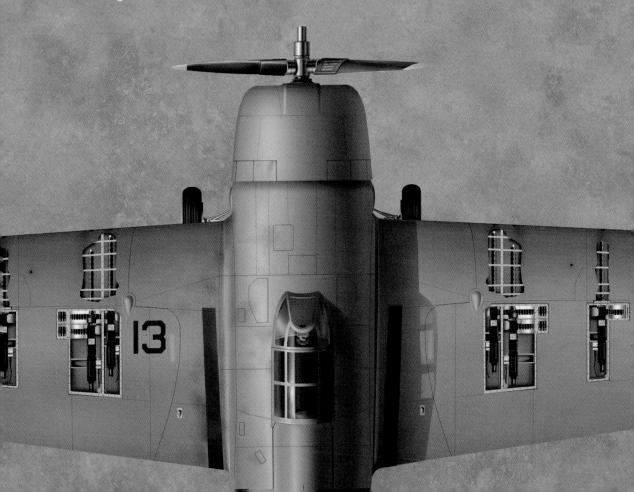

A6M ZERO-SEN

A6M1

The first two prototypes of the Zero-sen were initially referred to as 12-shi Carrier Fighters, but they eventually became A6M1s. The prototypes were powered by the Mitsubishi Zuisei-13 engine with a rating of 875hp.

The A6M1 set the basic configuration of the Zero-sen. Its fuselage was built in two sections, with the forward part being attached to the wing structure – the top of the wing served as the cockpit floor. While building the wing and forward fuselage as one integral section saved weight, it made construction more time-consuming and repair and maintenance more difficult. If part of the wing received major damage, the entire wing had to be replaced. The forward fuselage section ended at the aft end of the cockpit canopy and the trailing edge of the wing, the rear fuselage section beginning at this point. Both forward and rear sections were built using stressed-skin, semi-monocoque construction. The wings contained two 51.5-gallon fuel tanks, with an additional 38-gallon tank placed ahead of the cockpit. The main landing gear, tail wheel and arrestor hook were all fully retractable.

The pilot entered the airplane from the left side of the fuselage via three retractable steps and two handgrips, all carefully fitted for aerodynamic smoothness. Jiro Horikoshi and his team placed the cockpit high on the fuselage to give excellent all-around vision in combat. The cockpit itself was compact. The pilot's seat was adjustable up and down, but not forward – instead, the rudder pedals could be moved forward or backward. The arrangement of the instruments and controls followed conventional practice, with the exception of the gun controls. On the Zero-sen the gun selector and the firing button were placed on the throttle control, not on the control stick as in most other fighters.

The armament of the Zero-sen represented a sharp break with tradition. Definition of the requirements for the proposed 12-shi Carrier Fighter took place at a time when many of the world's air forces were reconsidering the efficacy of the standard armament of two rifle caliber machine guns – a hangover from World War I. Alternatives then under development were multiple batteries of rifle-caliber machine guns or weapons of a larger size. Recognizing the need for more powerful armament to deal with larger and stronger all-metal airplanes, the Imperial Japanese Navy's research program led to the decision to bypass the standard 7.7mm machine gun and adapt the 20mm cannon for fitment to the new fighter.

The IJNAF duly purchased a license to build the Oerlikon FF aircraft cannon in Japan. This became the Type 99-1 cannon, which traded a low muzzle velocity and rate-of-fire for light weight. This made it ideal for the planned new carrier fighter. The prototype and production models of the Zero-sen contained a short-barrel Type 99-1 cannon in each wing, equipped with a drum magazine containing 60 rounds of 20mm ammunition. Two 7.7mm machine guns were placed on the top of the fuselage to fire through the propeller, each gun having a magazine containing 500 rounds of ammunition. A selector switch on the throttle enabled the pilot to fire the machine guns or the cannon separately, or all four weapons together.

Although clearly less powerful than the 20mm cannon, the 7.7mm machine guns were still considered to be valuable for close-in fighting, where a Zero-sen pilot could use his airplane's superior maneuverability to close with his opponent to deliver a telling strike against the pilot or the fuel tanks of the enemy airplane. The greater explosive power of the 20mm cannon would enable the Zero-sen to deal effectively with larger aircraft threatening the fleet. This seemingly powerful armament proved to be less effective in combat than the IJNAF had hoped, however.

A6M2 MODEL 11

Adoption of the more powerful Nakajima Sakae-12 engine for the production versions of the A6M led to a change in designation to A6M2. With the Sakae engine, the maximum speed increased to 331mph. The A6M2 incorporated several minor modifications. Moving the vertical tail farther aft added 11 inches to the length of the fuselage, while the span of the horizontal tail surfaces was increased by four inches and raised 7.4 inches above the fuselage centerline. The air scoop for the Sakae engine's carburetor was relocated to the bottom of the engine cowling – a distinctive feature of the A6M2.

After the IJNAF's formal acceptance of the A6M2, the new fighter became the Type 0 Carrier Fighter Model 11, shortened to Reisen (Zero-sen Fighter). The first digit in the model number indicated changes in the airframe and the second digit changes in the engine. Mitsubishi built 64 Model 11 fighters.

The Model 11 was the first version to see combat when 15 aircraft were sent to the 12th Kokutai for operational testing. Additional Model 11s were sent to China to augment the IJNAF's fighter force, operating from land bases.

A6M2 MODEL 21

Carrier trials apparently indicated that even though the Zero-sen was within the specified wingspan, the airplane was a tight fit on the standard aircraft carrier elevator. To remove the chance of accidental damage to the wings, Mitsubishi designed a simple mechanism to fold the outer 20 inches of the wing vertically, reducing the wingspan

The Type 0 Model 21 was the IJNAF's workhorse during the first year of the Pacific War, serving with carrier and land-based air groups alike. Bearing two vertical stripes on its fuselage and an 'X' prefixed serial at the top of its tail fin, this Model 21 was one of 21 Zero-sens flown to Rabaul by the 3rd Kokutai in September 1942. (via Aerospace Publishing)

to just under 36ft. The IJNAF rejected the idea of incorporating a greater degree of wing folding due to the weight penalty it would have imposed. The modified wing configuration led to a change in model number, the revised airplane becoming the Model 21. The Type 0 Model 21 replaced the A5M Type 96 Carrier Fighter within IJNAF carrier- and land-based air groups as production at Mitsubishi and Nakajima built up. Ironically, the Nakajima Company would ultimately build more Zero-sens than Mitsubishi.

A significant difference between the carrier- and land-based versions of the Model 21 was the provision of a radio. The quality of Japanese airborne radio technology at the beginning of the Pacific War was barely adequate for air-to-air and air-to-ground communications, lacking both clarity in communication and range. For carrier fighters radio was clearly a necessity, even if poor quality, but in some land-based Zero-sen units the pilots removed the radios, viewing the equipment as so much useless weight.

A6M3 MODEL 32

As IJNAF pilots gained experience with the Zero-sen in combat over China and through continued testing, complaints and recommendations began to come in to the Kōku Hombu and to Mitsubishi. The most vocal complaint concerned the fighter's poor lateral control at high speeds. As air speed increased above 180mph, aileron response deteriorated rapidly, and above 230mph the Zero-sen became difficult to roll. Additionally, pilots wanted better performance at altitude and more ammunition for the Type 99-1 cannon.

In response, in mid-1941 Mitsubishi fitted two standard A6M2 airplanes with the improved Sakae-21 engine, which featured a two-stage, two-speed supercharger and a higher rating of 1,130hp. Slightly longer and heavier than the Sakae-12, the Sakae-21 required a new engine cowling, with openings in the front for the two 7.7mm machine guns, and a revised carburetor air scoop. After initial test flights pilots recommended eliminating the wing-folding mechanism and fairing over the wingtips. In shortening the wing by around three feet, the Mitsubishi engineers also shortened the ailerons. This combination improved aileron control, roll rates and the fighter's performance in a dive at higher speeds for a relatively small loss in overall maneuverability and rate-of-climb.

The ammunition feed system for the Type 99-1 cannon was changed from a drum magazine to a belt feed and the number of rounds increased to 100.

With both a revised fuselage and a new engine, the A6M3 was designated the Type 0 Carrier Fighter Model 32. Disappointingly, the Zero-sen Model 32 proved to be only marginally faster than the Zero-sen Model 21, due in part to the added weight of the new engine and more ammunition. More critically, although the capacity of the two wing fuel tanks was increased slightly, a reduction in the size of the fuselage fuel tank reduced the overall fuel capacity. As the Sakae-21 had higher fuel consumption than the Sakae-12, this reduced the Zero-sen Model 32's range.

Entering production in early 1942, the Zero-sen Model 32 went into action over New Guinea and the Solomon Islands later in the year.

A6M2 ZERO-SEN MODEL 21 COWLING/WING GUNS

The A6M2 Zero-sen Model 21 had two 7.7mm Type 97 machine guns mounted in the upper fuselage decking synchronized to fire through the propeller. Each machine gun was fed belted ammunition held in a fuselage-mounted box that contained 500 rounds. The Type 97 had a decent rate-of-fire, but against the more ruggedly built Wildcat the 7.7mm rounds were less effective – an F4F could absorb a considerable amount of damage and still make it home. The Model 21 had two Type 99-1

20mm cannon in the wings. Based on the Oerlikon FF, this was an exceptionally light weapon, but had a low rate-of-fire and a low muzzle velocity. IJNAF fighter pilots also complained about the limited amount of ammunition carried in the Zero-sen's wing magazines – each weapon fitted in the Model 21 had a drum housing just 60 rounds, which gave less than ten seconds worth of firing time at a rate of around 540 rounds per minute. The Zero Model 32 increased the load to 100 rounds.

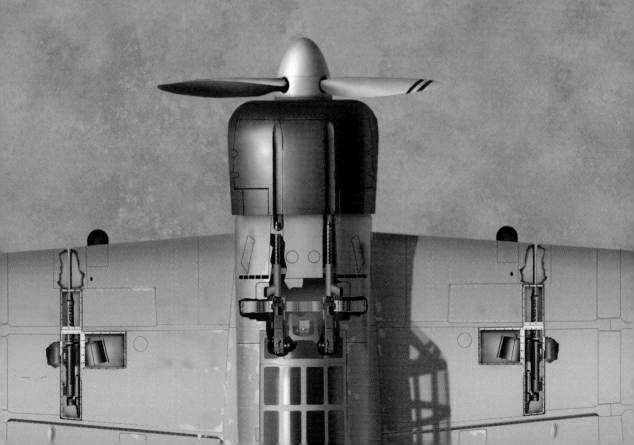

The Type 0 Model 32, which entered service during 1942, attempted to address the need for better performance at altitude and control at high speed. Note its clipped wingtips – the most visible distinguishing feature of the Model 32. (Peter M. Bowers Collection, Museum of Flight)

F4F-4 Wildcat and A6M2 Type 0 Carrier Fighter Model 21 Comparison Specifications

	F4F Wildcat	A6M2 Type 0 Model 21
Powerplant	1,200hp Pratt & Whitney R-1830-86	950hp Nakajima Sakae-12
Dimensions		
Span	38ft	39ft 4.7in.
Length	28ft 9in.	28ft 8in.
Height	11ft 1in.	10ft
Wing area	260sq. ft	241.5sq. ft
Weights		
Empty	5,766lb	3,704lb
Loaded	7,964lb	5,313lb
Performance		
Max speed	318mph at 19,400ft	331mph at 14,930ft
Range	830 miles	1,160 miles
Climb	to 10,000ft in 5 min 40 sec	to 19,685ft in 7 min 27 sec
Service ceiling	33,700ft	32,810ft
Armament	6 x 0.50in. M-2 Browning machine guns	2 x 7.7mm Type 97 machine guns and 2 x 20mm Type 99-1 cannon

THE STRATEGIC SITUATION

Japan went to war on December 7, 1941 to oust the Western colonial powers from Southeast Asia and gain control of the region's resources – food for the Japanese people, raw materials for Japan's war industries and, above all, oil for the IJN. In a carefully planned and brilliantly executed campaign, the Imperial Japanese Army and Navy effectively conquered all of Southeast Asia in a little over five months. By the end of April 1942, Japan's conquests stretched from the Kurile Islands in the north, across the Central Pacific, with footholds in the Bismarck Archipelago and New Guinea, through the Netherlands East Indies to the Andaman Islands in the Bay of Bengal and to the border between India and Burma. This was an achievement that astonished the Western powers.

The IJNAF's Zero-sen was in the vanguard of the assault. Using the fighter's exceptional range, the 3rd and Tainan Kokutais flew from their bases in Taiwan to engage American airplanes over Luzon, in the Philippines – a distance of more than 500 miles. Zero-sens detached from these units assisted the invasion of Malaya and participated in air attacks on Singapore and during the occupation of Sumatra, while their parent units advanced through the Netherlands East Indies, leapfrogging from captured airfield to captured airfield. Following the attack on Pearl Harbor, the carrier-based Zero-sen units assisted in the capture of Rabaul, on New Britain, and Lae, in New Guinea, and flew strikes against targets in Java, before attacking Darwin, on Australia's northern coast, and participating in the raid on British naval bases in Ceylon in early April 1942.

In the air battles over Southeast Asia, American, British and Dutch fighter airplanes and fighter pilots proved to be no contest for the experienced IJNAF Zero-sen pilots

Type O Model 21s belonging to the Yamada Unit of the 22nd Kōkū Sentai (22nd Air Flotilla) at Kota Bharu, in Malaya, in early 1942. The Yamada Unit consisted of one Chutai drawn from the 3rd Kōkutai and one from the Tainan Kōkutai. (P00618_001, Australian War Memorial)

and their exceptional fighter. Flying inferior aircraft, lacking combat experience and using tactics that played to the Zero-sen's strengths, many young Allied fighter pilots paid with their lives when they tried to dogfight with a Japanese machine. The Zero-sen's superlative maneuverability and the skills of its pilots shocked many. Seeming to have come from nowhere, the Zero-sen quickly gained a reputation as a nearly invincible "wonder airplane," at least in the opinion of the Western press.

The Japanese attack on Pearl Harbor caught the US Navy preparing for war, but by no means ready. On July 20, 1940, President Franklin Roosevelt signed a $4 billion Two-Ocean Navy appropriations bill authorizing a 70 percent increase in authorized tonnage, including the construction of 18 aircraft carriers, and a build-up to 15,000 aircraft by 1946. The US Navy had begun to expand its pilot force in 1939, but by 1941 the enlarged training program was still ramping up. On the eve of war the US Navy had 4,112 officer and enlisted pilots while the US Marine Corps had 505. The US Navy's pilots were spread among seven fleet aircraft carriers, one small escort carrier and five patrol wings, in addition to other shore establishments, while the US Marine Corps pilots were allocated to two Marine air wings (MAWs).

On December 7, 1941, the US Navy had approximately 157 F4F-3/3A Wildcats distributed among eight fighter squadrons, training units and aircraft pools in the Atlantic and Pacific Fleets, and 57 F4F-3/3As in three Marine Corps fighter squadrons in the 1st and 2nd MAWs.

The overwhelming speed and sweep of the Japanese advance created multiple strategic challenges for the US military. War Plan Orange, the pre-war joint Army-Navy plan for a potential conflict with Japan, had envisioned an offensive through the Central Pacific to capture the Caroline and Marshall Islands en route to Japan. The Japanese seizure of the Netherlands East Indies and positions in the Bismarck Archipelago and New Guinea now threatened Australia and New Zealand. The South Pacific had not figured in American pre-war planning, but it now became vital to defend Australia and to secure the shipping routes from the USA.

Although agreeing to a strategy of "Germany First," President Roosevelt and the American Joint Chiefs committed US forces to the defense of Australia and New Zealand in the early months of the war, and agreed to send reinforcements of troops, aircraft and ships to the South Pacific. However, lacking adequate ships, men and aircraft, there was little the US Navy could do to mount a determined resistance to the Japanese onslaught during the early months of 1942. Instead, during February and March, the Pacific Fleet's aircraft carriers conducted a series of lightning raids in the Central and Southwest Pacific, striking Japanese targets in the Marshall and Gilbert Islands, on Wake and Marcus Islands, at Lae and Salamaua, in New Guinea, and Rabaul, on New Britain.

Japan's strategy was to create a defensive barrier around its newly conquered territories to repel the inevitable American and British counteroffensives. Japan had no hope of defeating the United States in a protracted war of attrition. Instead, the Japanese leadership believed that by employing its superior military skill and spirit along interior lines of defense Japan could fight US forces to exhaustion and break America's will.

As Australia was the likely base for an American counteroffensive, strengthening the Japanese position in the South Pacific seemed imperative. In January the Japanese seized Rabaul, on the island of New Britain, to prevent its use as an Allied base for operations against the main Japanese stronghold at Truk. The IJN wanted to create a defense in depth around Rabaul by seizing Lae, Salamaua and Port Moresby, in eastern New Guinea, and Tulagi, in the Solomon Islands. From these bases Japanese airplanes could attack Australia.

The IJN also made plans for further advances beyond the Solomons to New Caledonia and Samoa to disrupt the line of communications between Australia and the United States. However, Adm Isoroku Yamamoto, commander of the IJN's

Re-arming an F4F-3 on board *Enterprise* during February–March 1942. (80G-63340, RG 80, NARA)

New F4F-4 Wildcats on the deck of *Enterprise* shortly before the Battle of Midway. By the end of May, all the fighter squadrons on *Enterprise, Yorktown* and *Hornet* had been re-equipped with the F4F-4. (80G-14120, RG 80, NARA)

Combined Fleet, argued instead for the vital necessity of completing the destruction of the US Navy's Pacific Fleet, especially its aircraft carriers. Rather than concentrating their forces against one objective, however, the Japanese chose to pursue both. By mid-April the Kaigun (Navy of the Greater Japanese Empire) had committed itself to Operation *MO* – the invasion of Port Moresby and the island of Tulagi, in the Solomons, in early May as a preliminary step to further operations in the South Pacific – and, in early June, Operation *MI*. The latter targeted Midway and the Aleutian Islands in an effort to further expand the defensive barrier in the Central Pacific and confront the American carriers.

Once US Naval Intelligence became aware of Japanese intentions in the South Pacific, Adm Ernest King, Chief of Naval Operations and Commander-in-Chief US Fleet, and Adm Chester Nimitz, Commander-in-Chief Pacific Fleet and Pacific Ocean Areas, decided to contest the Japanese advance on Port Moresby, thus setting the stage for what became the Battle of the Coral Sea. On May 7–8, 1942, in the first naval battle in history where the opposing ships never sighted each other, the US Navy sank the light carrier *Shōho* and damaged the *Shōkaku*, but lost the USS *Lexington* (CV-2). Although the Battle of the Coral Sea was a tactical victory for the Japanese, it ultimately proved to be a strategic loss. The island of Tulagi, in the Solomons, was indeed captured, but without carrier protection for the invasion force, the planned capture of Port Moresby had to be abandoned by the Japanese. The battle also deprived Adm Yamamoto of two of his most powerful carriers, the *Shōkaku* and the *Zuikaku*, a month before the advance on Midway.

US Marine Corps fighter squadron VMF-212 was one of the small number of units sent out to defend the islands in the Pacific along the route from the USA to Australia. VMF-212's aggressive leader, Maj Harold Bauer, stands just to the right of the squadron sign. (80G-357147, RG 80, NARA)

As is well known, the Battle of Midway marked the end of Japanese plans for expansion in the Central Pacific and Yamamoto's hopes for a decisive battle against the remaining American carriers. The loss of the four Japanese fleet carriers *Akagi, Kaga, Soryu* and *Hiryu* (the core of the Combined Fleet's striking power) on June 4, 1942 was a severe blow. The US Navy had suffered as well, losing USS *Yorktown* (CV-5) – the second fleet carrier sunk in the space of one month – and 80 carrier aircraft.

The Battles of the Coral Sea and Midway had seen the first confrontations between the F4F Wildcat and the Zero-sen. In air combat the Japanese fighter had proven to be faster, far more maneuverable and in possession of a better rate-of-climb than the Wildcat, but the latter's stronger construction, armor protection, self-sealing fuel tanks and more effective armament enabled the F4F pilots to begin to take the measure of the Zero-sen. At Coral Sea and Midway, US Navy pilots quickly began developing tactics to counter the Zero-sen's advantages.

In the aftermath of Midway both sides, for different reasons, renewed their focus on the South Pacific. The Japanese losses at Midway forced a cancellation of the plans to advance against New Caledonia and Samoa, but increased the importance of seizing Port Moresby and strengthening their position in the Solomon Islands in order to exert control over the Coral Sea. The Japanese Army and Navy agreed on an overland advance against Port Moresby, capturing Buna and its airfield on July 21 to serve as a jumping-off point.

As air support for the operation, the IJNAF had the 5th Kōkū Kūshū Butai (the 5th Air Attack Force, with the administrative title of the 25th Air Flotilla), consisting of the Tainan Kokutai (Type 0 Model 21s), the 4th Kokutai (Type 1 Medium Bombers) and the newly activated 2nd Kokutai (Type 0 Model 32 Fighters and Type 99 Carrier Bombers). These units were operating out of Rabaul and Lae, in New Guinea. At the same time, the IJNAF decided to build an air base on the island of Guadalcanal to extend the reach of Japanese air power. After preliminary surveys, two construction battalions arrived on Guadalcanal in early July to begin work on an airfield.

Henderson Field on Guadalcanal. The building in the background was dubbed "The Pagoda" and served as headquarters for the 1st MAW until it was destroyed in October 1942. (80G-20673, RG 80, NARA)

For some months Adm King had been urging an offensive against the Solomon Islands to protect the US–Australia line of communications and to serve as a base for an assault on Rabaul. In late June the Joint Chiefs agreed to King's plan to seize the Japanese base at Tulagi and the nearby Santa Cruz Islands. When intelligence reports reached them that the Japanese had started construction of an airfield on Guadalcanal, King immediately switched the objective from the Santa Cruz Islands to Guadalcanal, with a target date of August 1, 1942 for the invasion. In the event, the 1st Marine Division landed on Tulagi and Guadalcanal on August 7. Thus began a six-month campaign for control of the island that turned into a grinding battle of attrition involving five major naval surface actions, two carrier battles (the Battle of the Eastern Solomons and the Battle of Santa Cruz), three major Japanese land offensives and a sustained air campaign against US Marine Corps, US Navy, and USAAF airplanes based on Guadalcanal.

The battle for Guadalcanal was the first test of Japan's strategy of fighting American forces to the point of exhaustion. While the Japanese came perilously close to success on several occasions, in the end they failed.

This airfield at Rabaul looks just as sparse as Henderson Field in this panoramic view of the facilities "enjoyed" by the Tainan Kokutai during the ill-fated Guadalacanal campaign. Also an important staging area for IJNAF aircraft heading to other airfields in the Solomons, the facilities at Rabaul were used as central bases for satellite strips at Lae (New Guinea) and Buin (Bougainville). (via Henry Sakaida)

THE COMBATANTS

The battles between the Grumman Wildcat and the Mitsubishi Zero-sen during 1942 brought together the best of the IJNAF's and the US Navy's pre-war aviators – what historian John Lundstrom has called the US Navy's "First Team," and their US Marine Corps counterparts. In both navies these were men of considerable flying experience and, in the case of many of the Japanese pilots, combat service in China. A number were professional officers, graduates of their respective naval academies, but many more had come into flying through other recruitment paths. Their training had been rigorous and they had had to meet high standards of performance to gain their wings. They were well versed in fighter tactics, confident in their abilities and their aircraft. Later in that first year of the war younger, less experienced pilots who had been rushed through more abbreviated training programs joined the surviving pre-war pilots in the maelstrom of combat over the South Pacific.

IJNAF PILOT TRAINING

A fundamental difference between IJNAF and US Navy pilot training in the years leading up to World War II centered on contrasting philosophies with respect to military manpower. US armed forces traditionally relied on a core of trained professionals who maintained a small military force in peacetime, backed by a reserve force, and who in war would lead a greatly expanded military mobilized from the civilian population. The IJN, in contrast, adopted a philosophy of "quality over quantity" in both peace and war, creating a limited cadre of exceptionally well-trained and experienced officers and men equipped with superior weapons.

The Yokosuka K5Y Type 93 Intermediate Trainer, nicknamed "akatombo" (red dragonfly) because of its red training colors, was familiar to all IJNAF pilots. (via the author)

This philosophy was in tune with the IJN's obsession with the "Decisive Battle" concept – the view that one supreme engagement would decide the outcome of any war. The IJN planned for a short, victorious war, not a war of attrition. As a result of this philosophy, up until shortly before the outbreak of the Pacific War the IJNAF lacked the infrastructure for mass pilot and aircrew training. Its existing pilot training scheme was selective in the extreme, producing a very small number of exceptional pilots who represented only a fraction of those considered eligible.

The IJNAF drew its pilots from three sources. A small number of officer pilots came from the IJN Academy at Eta Jima, and they were duly trained in their own separate classes for eight months to a year. The vast majority of IJNAF pilots – upwards of 90 percent – were non-commissioned officers and enlisted men. Many came from within the ranks of the IJN through a highly selective and competitive examination process. The IJNAF also recruited young men directly from the civilian world through the so-called Yokaren (Flight Reserve) programs. The initial program set up in the early 1930s recruited boys aged 15 to 17, who were given three years of education and flight training. In 1937 the IJNAF began a new program to recruit young men who had completed three-and-a-half years of their middle school education, thereby reducing the time spent before they commenced flight training to 18 months. This subsequently became the largest source of aviation cadets.

During their pre-flight training the students were regularly subjected to strict regimentation, frequent corporal punishment and demanding physical activities. In 1940 the training programs for enlisted men were revised and flight training standardized (see Osprey Warrior 55 – *Imperial Japanese Naval Aviator 1937–45* for a more detailed description of these programs).

Prior to 1940, the flying training program lasted seven to nine months and covered primary and intermediary instruction. In the primary phase, trainees began instruction on the Yokosuka K2Y1/2 Primary Trainer, before moving on to the Yokosuka K5Y1/2 Type 93 Intermediate Trainer. Practice included the usual basic flying skills, aerobatics, formation flying, instrument flying and cross-country navigational exercises. After accumulating around 100 flying hours, and completing comprehensive examinations on their flying skills, trainees were assigned to a specialized airplane type (fighters, dive-bombers, torpedo-bombers multi-engined bombers, etc.) and began their advanced training program, lasting around three months. Neophyte fighter pilots joined the Saeki, Omura or Oita Kokutais for training in older operational aircraft, flying the Nakajima A2N Type 90 and A4N Type 95 Carrier Fighters, before moving on to the Mitsubishi A5M Type 96 Carrier Fighter when the Type 0 replaced it in frontline units.

During their advanced training, students received another 100–150 flying hours, when they were introduced to combat tactics and basic combat maneuvers, aerial gunnery, more formation flying and aerobatics in heavier and more powerful operational aircraft. Upon completion of their entire training program enlisted pilots would have accumulated around 250–300 flying hours and officer pilot trainees around 400 hours. After 1940, as the IJNAF began to expand its training program, the length of the latter was reduced to ten months to increase the output of trained pilots.

IJNAF student pilots prepare for a lesson in the A5M4-K advanced fighter trainer. The Mitsubishi A5M4-K was a two-seat version of the Type 96 Carrier Fighter that supplemented older operational types during basic combat training. (via the author)

After joining a tactical unit, the newly-graduated pilots continued their training. Up until the outbreak of the Pacific War the IJNAF's tactical units served the same function as operational training units. This was not necessarily a burden as new pilots were often assigned to new units forming in Japan. The new pilots undertook an intensive training program to refine the combat skills they had begun to learn during their advanced training course. Working with their more experienced colleagues, they practiced combat tactics, combat formations, gunnery and, for the carefully selected few, carrier operations. Only the very best pilots were selected for the carrier air groups – these were the IJNAF's elite, the "best of the best."

During the war in China, newer pilots could be gradually broken into combat and carefully shepherded by the veterans in the air group. In his memoir *Samurai!*, future high-scoring ace Saburo Sakai recalled how he was assigned to flying close air support missions for the Japanese Army for several weeks before he was allowed to join the veterans on combat air patrols.

The IJNAF's pilot training system was successful in producing a relatively small number of superbly trained and exceptionally skilled flyers. In December 1941, the IJN went to war with approximately 3,500 pilots, of which some 600 were assigned to the carrier air groups. They had an average of between 600 and 800 flying hours, and many benefited from having seen combat in China. But there was no real reserve of pilots, and as nearly every unit became heavily involved in combat duties, there was little time to perform the operational training role for newly assigned pilots.

During 1941 the IJNAF developed a plan to train upwards of 15,000 pilots a year, but with the outbreak of the war this plan fell by the wayside. The training system was subsequently expanded to produce around 2,000 pilots a year, but events would prove that this was not enough. As Mitsuo Fuchida and Masatake Okumiya (both formerly IJN officers) wrote in their history of the Battle of Midway, the IJN high command "failed to realize that aerial warfare is a battle of attrition, and that a strictly limited number of even the most skillful pilots could not possibly win out over an unlimited number of able pilots."

1. Clock
2. Cylinder head temperature gauge
3. Rudder pedal adjustment levers
4. Propeller control
5. Ignition switch
6. Propeller selector switch
7. Emergency electrical fuel pump switch
8. Check-off switch
9. Carburetor air control
10. Altimeter
11. Directional gyro
12. Padded electrical Mk 8 gunsight
13. Airspeed indicator
14. Turn-and-bank indicator
15. Rate-of-climb indicator
16. Gyro horizon
17. Manifold pressure gauge
18. Tachometer
19. Outside air temperature gauge
20. Fuel quantity gauge
21. Primer pump
22. Cowl flaps hand crank
23. Engine temperature gauge
24. Compass
25. Oil dilution switch
26. Radio signal light
27. Electric wiring diagram
28. Fuel tank selector valve
29. Rudder tab control
30. Aileron tab control
31. Throttle control
32. Recognition lights switches
33. Mixture control
34. Elevator tab control
35. Arrestor hook control
36. Starter switch
37. Tailwheel castor lock
38. Friction adjusting knob
39. Gunsight light rheostat
40. Electrical distribution panel and switch box
41. Fuse panel (spare fuses and bulbs under door)
42. Gun charging handle
43. Landing gear handcrank
44. Electric circuit breaker reset buttons
45. Control column
46. Pilot seat
47. Pilot seat belts
48. Cockpit lighting
49. Rudder pedals
50. Fire extinguisher switch

A6M2 ZERO-SEN COCKPIT

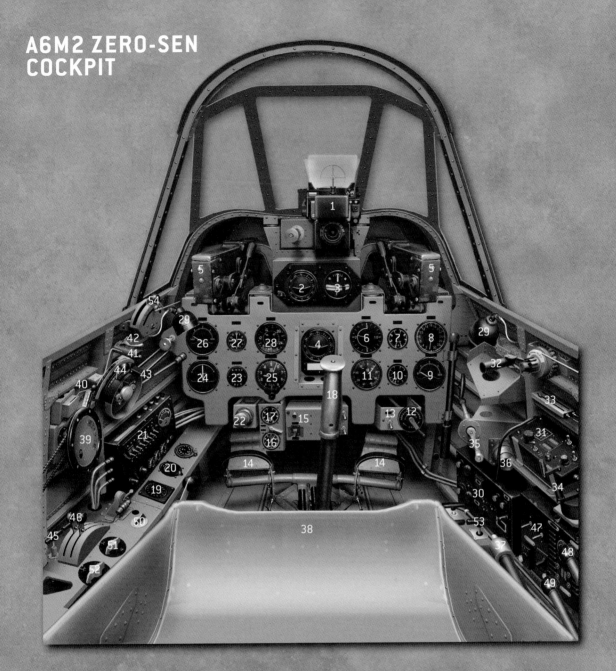

1. IJNAF Type 98 Reflector Gunsight
2. Artificial horizon
3. Turn-and-bank indicator
4. Compass
5. IJNAF Type 97 7.7mm machine guns
6. Rate-of-climb indicator
7. Fuel pressure gauge
8. Tachometer
9. Cylinder head temperature gauge
10. Oil temperature gauge
11. Intake manifold pressure gauge
12. Oil cooler shutter control handle
13. Ignition plug charger switch
14. Brake pedals
15. Oxygen control
16. Oxygen pressure gauge
17. Oxygen quantity gauge
18. Control column
19. Wing fuel tank quantity gauge
20. Fuselage fuel tank quantity gauge
21. Switchboard
22. Fuel injection pump
23. Engine main switch
24. Radio direction indicator
25. Altimeter
26. Exhaust temperature gauge
27. Clock
28. Airspeed indicator
29. Interior lights
30. Radio homing control unit
31. Type 3 Mk 1 Radio Control panel
32. Arrestor hook retraction handle
33. Arrestor hook/flap down angle indicator
34. Radio homing equipment control lever
35. Cowl gills control handle
36. Cockpit ventilation air intake
37. Seat adjustment lever
38. Seat
39. Elevator trim tab control handle
40. Machine gun safety lever
41. Throttle lever
42. Machine gun selector switch
43. Propeller pitch adjustment lever
44. Mixture control lever
45. Drop tank release lever
46. Bomb release levers
47. Switchboard
48. Flap control
49. Landing gear lever
50. Wing tanks fuel gauge
51. Fuselage/wing tank switching cock
52. Wing tanks selector lever
53. Emergency gear down lever
54. High altitude automatic mixture control

US NAVY AND US MARINE CORPS PILOT TRAINING

The US Navy and the US Marine Corps recruited their pilots from two sources – the US Naval Academy and the Volunteer Naval Reserve class V-5 Naval Aviation Cadet program for civilian and enlisted candidates. Prior to 1939, Naval Aviation Cadets who had come in through the V-5 program undertook 18 months of training and served for three years on active duty as Naval Aviators with the rank of Aviation Cadet, after which they were eligible for promotion to Lieutenant in the US Navy Reserve. In June 1939 Congress amended the program to allow for Aviation Cadets to receive immediate commissions as Ensigns or Second Lieutenants after 12 months of training.

Non-US Navy candidates for the V-5 program went to one of 13 Naval Reserve Bases around the country for initial evaluation. These so-called elimination bases evaluated prospective candidates and their potential for completing pilot training. Candidates received physical training, were taught basic military skills and Navy customs, but most importantly received ten hours of flight training leading to a solo flight. Having successfully passed these tests, the prospective candidates went on to NAS Pensacola, Florida, for flight training. Naval Academy graduates went directly to Pensacola after completing a period of service at sea.

Up to October 1939, with a relatively small number of airplanes and pilots authorized for the US Navy's aviation branch, the goal of the US Navy's aviation training was to give its prospective pilots instruction in how to fly all types of naval aircraft. After completing 33 weeks of ground school, the trainees spent a year working their way through Pensacola's five training squadrons.

US Navy and US Marine Corps pilots began their flight training on biplane primary trainers, either the Naval Aircraft Factory N3N, nicknamed "The Yellow Peril," or the Stearman N2S, shown here. (Robert Lawson Collection, National Museum of Naval Aviation)

Students began with nine weeks in Squadron One flying primary seaplanes (the float-equipped version of the N3N biplane trainer), learning basic flying procedures, before progressing to Squadron Two and 18 weeks of flying primary land airplanes. Here, they would master aerobatics, formation flying, night flying and cross-country navigation. In their nine weeks in Squadron Three, the trainees flew more powerful, but second-line, operational airplanes like the Vought O3U and SBU and the new SNJ trainer, developing the skills they had mastered in Squadron Two and beginning to work on instrument flying. The trainees spent another nine weeks in Squadron Four, learning how to fly operational seaplanes and flying boats, before completing their training in Squadron Five. Here, they flew operational carrier airplanes and were instructed in aerial gunnery and combat tactics, dive- and torpedo-bombing and carrier landings.

By the end of a full year's training, students would have accumulated around 300 hours of flying time. After earning his wings of gold, a newly minted pilot would be qualified to be assigned to any US Navy carrier, observation or land-based squadron. With the shorter syllabus introduced after October 1939, trainees received around 200 hours of flying time.

Following President Franklin D. Roosevelt's declaration of a limited national emergency after the outbreak of the war in Europe in September 1939, the US Navy restructured its training syllabus in October to facilitate an immediate expansion of pilot training. From now on trainees would specialize in carrier, patrol/observation or utility aircraft. The ground school was cut to 18 weeks, and the flying training program reduced from a year to six months. Instead of going through all five training squadrons, trainees began with primary land airplanes in Squadron One to acquire basic flying skills, before moving on to basic service types in Squadron Two, where they were introduced to formation flying and instrument flying. After completing the Squadron Two syllabus, the trainees split off. Those assigned to carrier aircraft learned the basics of aerial combat, aerial gunnery and dive- and torpedo-bombing, before being assigned to active duty squadrons. Other trainees went on to multi-engined patrol airplanes or scouting and observation types, the latter operating from battleships and cruisers.

Three US Marine Corps F4F Wildcats flying over Quantico in May 1941. Up until July of that year, US Navy and US Marine Corps fighter squadrons, like their IJNAF counterparts, conducted much of the operational training for newly graduated fighter pilots, refining and honing the skills they had learned in advanced training through hours of practice. (127G-81Z-525772, RG 127, NARA)

The US Navy put heavy emphasis on air-to-air gunnery, and devoted many hours to training Naval Aviators in deflection shooting. This cover from a 1942 US Navy training manual summarizes the official approach taken to aerial gunnery. (via the author)

This new training framework enabled the US Navy to respond to the increase in authorized airplane strength to 15,000 machines under the Two-Ocean Navy Act. Planning for a long war, the US Navy began ramping up its training program. During 1941 the monthly quota of pilot trainees was increased from 800 to 2,500 a month.

Much like the IJNAF, the US Navy's squadrons had served as their own operational training units. In order to free squadrons from this responsibility, the US Navy authorized the formation of Advanced Carrier Training groups in July 1941 to provide additional training in operating the latest combat types, advanced aerial gunnery and advanced fighter tactics. New pilots received 75 to 150 hours of additional flight training at the ACTGs. In addition, to speed up the output of trained Naval Aviators, the requirement to have pilots capable of flying all three types of carrier aircraft was abolished. Students were now selected for fighters, dive-bombers or torpedo-bombers only, and trained on the type of aircraft they would fly when assigned to a carrier squadron.

Where the US Navy differed from other air services was its emphasis on aerial gunnery, particularly deflection shooting. The mission of the fighter pilot was the destruction of enemy aircraft, so the US Navy's objective was to train its fighter pilots in a routine designed to be simple and effortless, and have them practice this routine "until its performance becomes as automatic and instinctive as breathing in your sleep."

There were two key elements in the US Navy's approach – where to aim and when to fire. Fighter pilots were trained to aim at "a definite spot in space that will become full of enemy airplane when your bullets reach there" based on the speed and flightpath of their intended target and the speed and line of travel of their bullets. Having calculated the proper lead, or deflection, pilots were instructed to open fire 1,000ft from the target, but continue firing as they closed in to the best range of 200–300ft. Pilots were trained to fire with one-quarter, one-half, three-quarter and full deflection.

Once the principles of lead and range were absorbed, pilots received training on specific approaches to a target – from the side, from overhead, from head on and from the stern – and were taught to adapt their approach both to the type of aircraft they were attacking and the tactical situation at the time. After the theory came practice, practice and more practice until gunnery approaches became second nature. As a later gunnery manual advised new fighter pilots, these approaches were the basis for the laws of combat tactics, and the penalty for disobeying these laws was death.

COMBAT

IJNAF FIGHTER TACTICS

The basic combat unit in the IJNAF was the three-airplane shotai, which was a variation of the three-airplane V-formation consisting of a leader and two wingmen that was common to most of the world's air forces in the interwar period. While perfectly adequate for flying to and from a target, IJNAF fighter pilots found that in actual combat a tight V-formation was too rigid and less than effective. They duly developed a looser V-formation, with the wingmen flying further back and at different altitudes, instead of being tied closely to the leader.

In this revised combat formation, one wingman would fly 200 meters behind the leader and the second wingman around 300 meters behind, with one stepped up 200 meters in altitude and the second some 300 meters higher. In this formation the wingmen were not glued to the leader and concentrating on avoiding collisions. Instead, they could spend time scanning the sky for enemy aircraft. The shotai leader initiated the attack on an enemy aircraft or formation, and could deploy his wingmen in line astern or line abreast as the tactical situation required for sequential passes against the target.

While excelling at individual combat, during the first year of the Pacific War the Zero-sen pilots more often employed hit-and-run tactics against an enemy airplane, with each pilot in the shotai diving down to make an individual firing pass, pulling out underneath the enemy aircraft and climbing swiftly back up to altitude to regain the initiative. Alternatively, the leader could have one of the wingmen remain above the target as top cover (*text continues on page 52*).

49

JOSEPH FOSS

Capt Joe Foss was the top-scoring Wildcat pilot against the Zero-sen. Born in Sioux Falls, South Dakota, on April 17, 1915, he learned to fly while attending college, enlisting in the US Marine Corps in 1940 after graduation from the University of South Dakota. Foss did his flight training at NAS Pensacola, winning his wings and a commission as a Second Lieutenant in March 1941. To his intense frustration Foss was assigned as a Primary Instructor at Pensacola, after which he was posted to a reconnaissance squadron. He eventually talked his way into the Advanced Carrier Training Group, and after completing the course was promoted to Captain and made executive officer of VMF-121 in August 1942. By this time Foss had accumulated around 1,000 flying hours, which served him well in combat.

VMF-121 arrived on Guadalcanal on October 9, 1942. Four days later, on his fifth combat mission, Foss shot down his first Zero-sen, and then had a narrow escape when three more A6Ms badly shot up his Wildcat, forcing him to make a dead stick landing. Over the next six weeks Foss claimed 23 victories, including 16 Zero-sens. He learned not to open fire until he was as close as possible to his target – so close that one of his pilots supposedly accused him of leaving powder burns on the IJNAF fighters that he shot down. If they could, Foss and the other pilots tried to use high-speed hit-and-run tactics to avoid the Zero-sen's superior maneuverability, although many times they fought from a less than advantageous position. To conserve ammunition Foss often used only four of his six machine guns – more than enough to explode a Zero-sen at close range.

Foss claimed four Zero-sens shot down on October 23, 1942, returning to Guadalcanal once again in a shot-up Wildcat. Two days later he went one better when he claimed two Zero-sens during a morning mission and three more during the afternoon. He claimed his last victories – three more Zero-sens – on January 15, 1943 after VMF-121 had returned from leave in Australia. These last claims made Foss the first American pilot in World War II to equal Capt Eddie Rickenbacker's World War I record of 26 victories, and gave him a total of 19 Zero-sens shot down – the highest score of any US Marine Corps or US Navy Wildcat pilot against the Mitsubishi fighter. For his achievements during the Guadalcanal campaign Capt Joseph Foss was awarded the Congressional Medal of Honor on May 18, 1943.

Promoted to Major, Foss subsequently returned to combat as CO of VMF-115, but enjoyed no more aerial success. He went on to have a distinguished post-war career, serving several terms as Governor of his home state. Foss passed away on January 1, 2003.

YOSHIRO HASHIGUCHI

Yoshiro Hashiguchi is representative of the many enlisted pilots who comprised the core of the IJNAF's air groups during World War II. These men were trained in a hard school. Many were exceptional pilots, and fought tenaciously as the odds against them steadily worsened as the war progressed.

Hashiguchi was born in 1918 in Fukuoka City on the island of Kyushu, in southern Japan. He joined the IJN in 1937 and entered flying training through the Flight Reserve Enlisted Trainee program for non-commissioned officer personnel. Hashiguchi graduated in September 1938 as a member of the 42nd Class. He was one of 16 trainees selected to specialize in flying fighter aircraft. After completing his training Hashiguchi served with the Saeki, Oita and Omura Kokutai in Japan, flying the A5M Type 96 Carrier Fighter. In June 1939 Hashiguchi was posted to the 12th Kokutai based at Hankow, in China, where he flew Type 96 fighters until being wounded in October when Chinese Air Force bombers attacked his airfield. After recovering from his wounds Hashiguchi returned to Japan in January 1940 to join the Suzuka Kokutai as an instructor pilot.

In November 1941 Hashiguchi was assigned to the newly re-organized 3rd Kokutai. Established in April 1941 as a Type 1 Attack Bomber unit, the 3rd Kokutai was re-formed as a fighter unit in September and equipped with the A6M2 Type 0 Model 21 fighter. As part of the 11th Kōkū Kantai, the 3rd participated in the invasion of the Philippines and the Netherlands East Indies. Fighting against Dutch Brewster Buffaloes and Curtiss Hawk 75s and American P-40s, Hashiguchi achieved several victories, but was wounded again while strafing a radio station. He returned to combat in April 1942 when the 3rd Kokutai was operating against Darwin. In September the unit was transferred to Rabaul, and for the next two months Hashiguchi flew missions against US Marine Corps and US Navy Wildcats on Guadalcanal. On October 18, 1942 he was involved in an intense battle with F4Fs that ended with Hashiguchi and two other pilots in the shotai that he was leading claiming five fighters shot down. The 3rd Kokutai was finally withdrawn from Rabaul in November, returning to the Dutch East Indies.

Hashiguchi was sent back to Japan in June 1943, where he again instructed, before becoming a carrier fighter pilot with the 601st Kokutai aboard *Shōkaku* as the senior NCO pilot. Having survived the bloodbath of the First Battle of the Philippine Sea in June 1944, he transferred to the 653rd Kokutai embarked in the light carrier *Chiyoda*. Hashiguchi was posted missing in action during the Battle of Cape Egano off the Philippines on October 25, 1944 when his carrier was sunk with all hands. During nearly three years of combat he had accumulated at least ten, and possibly a few more, victories. He was not one of the IJNAF's leading aces, but he and the many other NCO pilots he flew with were the backbone of the IJN's fliers. Their victories were hard won through months of intensive, grueling air combat, and they fought on until almost all of them were killed. Of the 16 fighter pilots in the 42nd Class, Hashiguchi and 12 others were killed in action, and two more died in flying accidents.

The three-airplane Shotai was the IJNAF's basic combat unit, consisting of a leader and two wingmen. When employed by the Japanese, it was more flexible than the standard V-formation common to many of the world's air forces at that time. (via the author)

Defensively, the shotai provided mutual support. If attacked, the leader could pull up in a climbing turn, using the Zero-sen's fast climbing ability, while the wingmen came in against the attacking enemy fighter from different angles. If a Zero-sen pilot could draw an enemy fighter into a dogfight, a favorite tactic was the hineri-komi – a twisting maneuver the IJNAF pilot would execute at the top of a loop to come down on his opponent's tail, employing the Zero-sen's phenomenal maneuverability at low speeds.

To be effective in the turmoil of air combat the pilots within the shotai required superlative flying skills, exceptional coordination and an almost intuitive understanding and anticipation of the actions, or reactions, of the other members of the formation. This was especially true for the land-based Zero-sen fighter units, who often removed the radios from their aircraft. Perfecting this coordination came from hour after hour of relentless practice. The Zero-sen units that went to war in December 1941 benefited from having experienced pilots who had trained together for months.

The combination of pilot experience, the flexibility of the shotai formation and the performance of the Zero-sen proved too much for Allied fighter units encountered over the Philippines, Malaya and the Netherlands East Indies in early 1942. However, as attrition began to take its toll, newer replacement pilots came in who did not have the same levels of experience. With the Zero-sen units heavily involved in combat, there was less time to devote to training missions, where pilots could perfect their coordinated shotai tactics. Without radio communication, coordination of the formation with less well-trained pilots became more difficult. Although these formation tactics proved less adaptable to the realities of air combat over the South Pacific, the IJNAF took an inordinate amount of time to institute changes.

The IJNAF's fighter escort tactics were also a product of experience in China. The standard escort procedure that had been developed in the late 1930s was for the fighters to provide bombers with what was termed "direct cover." The fighters normally flew above and behind the bomber formation they were escorting. While this gave the fighters maximum flexibility to maneuver, in the air battles over Guadalcanal this tactic often meant the escorts were poorly placed to counter enemy fighters attacking the bomber formation. The inability of the bombers to communicate with their fighter escort, due to the lack of radios in the Zero-sens, compounded the problem. On some occasions the escorts would not be aware that their charges were under attack until they saw a burning Type 1 bomber falling from the sky.

US NAVY AND US MARINE CORPS FIGHTER TACTICS

During the inter-war period US Navy and the US Marine Corps fighter squadrons also used the V-formation of three aircraft as the basic tactical unit. With fighters flying at higher speeds and with larger turning circles, such a tactical unit became less effective as a combat formation as it prevented sharp radical turns and forced the two wingmen to spend too much time looking inward to avoid colliding with their leader rather than outward searching for enemy fighters.

Soon after the European War began, the US Navy began experimenting with a two-airplane formation that saw the leader designated as the attacker and the wingman protecting him from attack. Spacing between the two aircraft increased to around 150ft to allow for more freedom of movement, easier turns and keeping a sharp lookout for enemy airplanes. The US Navy designated two squadrons, VF-2 and VF-5, to experiment with the new formation. Reports from American observers in England reinforced the concept of the two-airplane section as the superior tactical formation. It took until mid-1941, however, for the US Navy to adopt the two-airplane element.

Fighter squadrons, which at the time had a complement of 18 aircraft, were divided into three divisions of six machines in three two-airplane sections, with the most senior pilot flying as the division leader. The sections would fly around 300ft apart in line astern or in an echelon formation behind the division leader. Approaching a formation of enemy aircraft, the division leader would assess the situation and determine the type of attack to be executed, ordering the three sections to engage the enemy in succession or separately as necessary. A section leader could employ one of the standard gunnery approaches, knowing that his wingman would be following behind guarding his tail. With more distance between aircraft, division and section leaders abandoned the hand signals of the open-cockpit era for radio and quick rocking of wings to alert others to an impending maneuver.

Introduction of the folding-wing F4F-4 in early 1942 enabled an increase in the number of aircraft in the carrier fighter squadrons from 18 to 27, but the units retained the six-airplane division. When combat losses or other missions limited the number of aircraft available, a squadron might send off a division of six fighters accompanied by a division of four, but always in sections of two machines.

There was one tactical innovation developed before the outbreak of war with Japan that was to prove invaluable in countering the Zero-sen fighter. In the spring of 1941, then Lt John Thach, commander of VF-3, came across an intelligence report on a new Japanese fighter aircraft with performance superior to the F4F-3s VF-3 was about to convert to. The report stated that the fighter had a superior rate-of-climb, higher speed

Lt (jg) John Kleinman sits on the wing of one of VF-5's F4F-4s, named "THE MOLE", on Guadalcanal in late September or early October 1942. By October 6, 1942 Kleinman had claimed two victories in aerial fighting over the island. (Robert Lawson Collection, National Museum of Naval Aviation)

The IJNAF's basic fighter
formation consisted of three
Zero-sens flying in a V-formation.
With combat experience,
Japanese pilots modified the
basic V into a looser formation,
with the wingmen staggered
above and behind the leader
to give the formation more
tactical flexibility and a better
lookout for enemy airplanes.

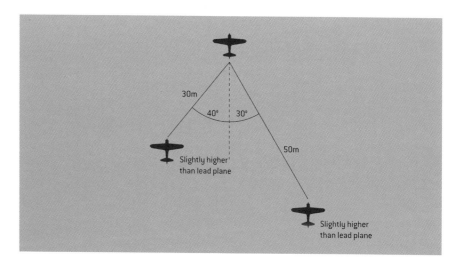

30m

40° 30°

Slightly higher
than lead plane

50m

Slightly higher
than lead plane

and the ability to out-turn any opponent. As Thach recalled in a post-war interview, "when I realized that this airplane, if this intelligence report were correct, had us beat in all three categories, it was pretty discouraging."

Some of his pilots refused to believe the report and thought it was a gross exaggeration, but Thach argued that even if it was only half true, the Japanese fighter would still be superior to the Wildcat. Thach believed he had to do something about this. Looking at the Wildcat, and the gunnery training his pilots had received, Thach believed they had one advantage. "We had good guns, and could shoot and hit even if we only had a fleeting second or two to take aim. Therefore, we had to do something to entice the opponent into giving us that one all important opportunity – it was the only chance we had."

Working at night at his kitchen table, using matches to represent airplanes, Thach experimented with different formations, trying out his ideas the next day using real airplanes. The key was to create that one opportunity to get in a killing burst of fire against an enemy opponent.

It was standard practice at the time to turn into an attacking enemy. Thach realized that if he placed two sections at a tactical distance from each other – that is, the

Lt Cdr John Thach, who as CO of
VF-3 during the Battle of Midway
successfully employed the
weaving tactic he had developed
to counter the Zero-sen's superior
maneuverability. (80G-64822,
RG 80, NARA)

distance equal to the diameter of their tightest turning circle – he could create the opportunity he was looking for by having both sections turn toward each other if one was attacked. If enemy aircraft made a stern attack on the section flying on the right, this section would quickly turn toward the section flying on the left, which would turn into the enemy attack and gain a head-on firing position. This also had the benefit of throwing off the enemy's attack, and presenting him with a more difficult full deflection shot. For the tactic to work, Thach used a division of four aircraft in two sections, instead of six aircraft.

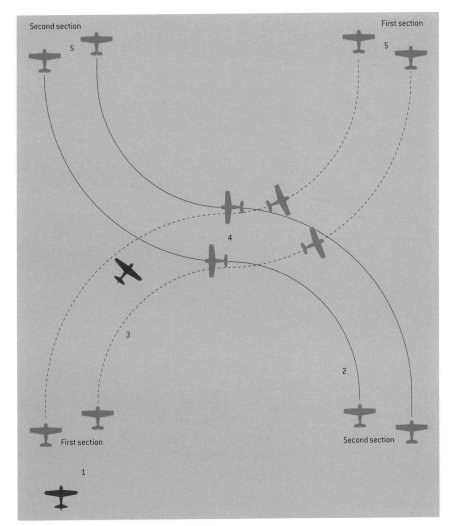

Lt Cdr John Thach developed this defensive tactic to counter the Zero-sen's superior maneuverability. When an IJNAF fighter (1) attacked a division of two elements (2) from the rear, the elements would turn sharply towards each other (4), giving the second element a head-on shot at the attacking Zero-sen (3). Dubbed the "Thach Weave," (5) this became the standard defensive tactic for Naval Aviators fighting against the Zero-sen.

Lt Cdr John Thach's defensive weave maneuver was based on a division of two elements flying in what he called the "Beam Defense Position," in line abreast at a distance equal to the Wildcat's turning radius. The "Beam Defense Position" and the "Thach Weave" could be used either by elements within a division of four aircraft, or by single airplanes in an element of two.

One of the advantages of the tactic was that it did not need radio communications between the two sections. Thach worked out a system whereby the section on the right looked out over the section on the left, and vice versa. If the right-hand section saw enemy aircraft coming in to attack the section on the left, they would immediately turn in on the left-hand section, which, seeing their colleagues initiating a turn, would immediately begin their turn to the right. The scissoring tactic could be used repeatedly to fend off enemy attacks.

The F4F-3 was the first model of the Wildcat to see combat with the Zero-sen fighter, during the Battle of the Coral Sea on May 7–8, 1942. (Peter M. Bowers Collection, Museum of Flight)

To test the tactic, Thach and three other pilots flew their fighters with their throttles retarded against other Wildcats flying at full throttle. It worked, time and again. The Beam Defense Position, as Thach named it, gave him and his pilots "something to work on, to keep us from being demoralized". At Midway, Thach got his chance to try out his tactic in the only school that really mattered.

CORAL SEA AND MIDWAY

The first clash between the Wildcat and the Zero-sen took place on May 7, 1942 over the Coral Sea. That morning strike groups from *Lexington* and *Yorktown* (Task Force 17) attacked the IJN's light carrier *Shōho*, whose aircraft were covering the Port Moresby invasion force. Lt Cdr James "Jimmy" Flatley led eight F4F-3s from VF-42 as escort for *Yorktown*'s VT-5 TBD Devastator torpedo-bombers. *Shōho* had sent up a combat air patrol of Type 96 and Type 0 fighters to defend the carrier.

As the Japanese pilots went after the torpedo-bombers, Flatley's division fell on them. Although the Wildcat pilots were astonished at the maneuverability of the fighters flown by their IJNAF opponents, Flatley managed to shoot down a Type 96 fighter and two of his pilots traded fire with a Zero-sen. Having climbed above the melee, Ens Walter Hass saw a Japanese fighter – one of three Zero-sens from *Shōho* – break away and head towards him. With the advantage of altitude, Hass dived on the unsuspecting fighter, getting in a solid burst that sent the Japanese airplane crashing into the sea below. Hass had just become the first US Navy or US Marine Corps pilot to shoot down a Zero-sen.

The next day search airplanes from Task Force 17 and the Japanese Striking Force (*Shōkaku* and *Zuikaku*) located their rival carrier forces and sent off strike groups to attack. *Yorktown*'s strike group went out first, with a division from VF-42 escorting the torpedo-bombers from VT-5 once again. *Lextington*'s strike group followed, with an escort of nine Wildcats from VF-2. Combat air patrols from *Shōkaku* and *Zuikaku* intercepted the American formations, and in the fighting that followed the Wildcat pilots claimed three Zero-sens shot down for the loss of three fighters. Following the attacks on the Striking Force, *Shōkaku*'s Zero-sen pilots claimed five Wildcats destroyed, while their counterparts aboard *Zuikaku* claimed no fewer than 13 F4F-3s shot down!

Shōkaku and *Zuikaku* sent out a combined force of 33 Type 99 Carrier Bombers, 18 Type 97 Attack Planes and an escort of 18 Zero-sen fighters to attack Task Force 17. VF-2 and VF-42 sent up 20 Wildcats on combat air patrol who engaged the IJNAF fighters in a series of fierce engagements at low and medium altitude, losing two Wildcat pilots killed in action and one fighter that had to ditch. Sections sometimes broke up in the heat of the action, and this resulted in Wildcat pilots repeatedly finding Zero-sens on their tails just as they positioned themselves to attack another Japanese fighter. This was an effective demonstration of the shotai tactics of mutual support. When faced with such a situation Wildcat pilots resorted to high-speed dives and cloud to escape their pursuers.

Lt Cdr "Jimmy" Flatley led his division in a hit-and-run attack against nine Zero-sens, claiming one shot down before the division broke up into individual combats. Flatley took on three fighters on his own in a hit-and-run attack, attempting to pull up into a firing position on one Zero-sen before diving away to escape. Flatley's wingman, Lt(jg) Richard Crommelin, claimed two fighters shot down, but it appears that none were actually lost in this fight.

One of the US Navy's great fighter leaders of World War II, Lt Cdr James "Jimmy" Flatley. After the Battle of the Coral Sea he began working out tactics to counter the Zero-sen. (80G-398396, RG 80, NARA)

US Navy Wildcat pilots came away from their first confrontations with the Zero-sen confident that they could take on the Japanese fighter and win, despite its obvious superiority over the F4F-3. As Lt Cdr Flatley stated in his after-action report, "The F4F-3 airplane properly handled can beat the enemy carrier-based fighters encountered so far. This includes type 'Zero'." Recognizing that the Zero-sen was far more maneuverable than the Wildcat, Flatley recommended tactics that could counter the fighter's advantage:

> The most effective attack against a more maneuverable fighter is to obtain altitude advantage, dive in, attack and pull up using speed gained in a dive to maintain altitude advantage. The old dogfight of chasing tails is not satisfactory and must not be employed when opposing Jap VF [fighter] planes.

Flatley distilled his experiences into eight points he termed "Hints To Navy VF Pilots":

1. Gain plenty of altitude before contact with enemy VF. You can lose altitude fast but you can't gain it fast enough when up against enemy VF.
2. Use hit-and-run attacks, diving in and pulling out and up. If your target maneuvers out of your sight during your approach pull out and let one of the following airplanes get him. If you attempt to twist and turn you will end up at his level or below, and will be unable to gain the advantage.
3. If you get in a tough spot dive away, maneuver violently, find a cloud.
4. Stay together. The Japs' air discipline is excellent, and if you get separated you will have at least three of them on you at once.
5. You have the better airplane if you handle it properly. In spite of their advantage in

maneuverability, you can and should shoot them down with few losses to yourselves. The reason for this is your greater firepower and more skillful gunnery.

6. Don't get excited and rush in. Take your time and make the first attack effective.

7. Watch out for ruses. The Japs have a method of creating smoke from their exhaust which doesn't mean a thing [this was apparently simply exhaust from acceleration]. Set them on fire before you take your guns off them.

8. Never hesitate to dive in. The hail of bullets around their cockpit will divert and confuse them, and will definitely cause them to break-off what they are doing and take avoiding action.

Upon returning home Flatley assumed command of VF-10 and prepared a short manual for his squadron titled "Combat Doctrine," encapsulating all his thinking on fighter tactics against enemy aircraft. Copies apparently circulated to other US Navy and US Marine Corps fighter squadrons on the West Coast. One pilot who pored over Flatley's manual on his way to the Southwest Pacific was the newly appointed Executive Officer of VMF-121, Capt Joseph Foss.

Less than a month after the Battle of the Coral Sea, Marine Corps Wildcat pilots on Midway and US Navy pilots aboard USS *Enterprise* (CV-6), *Hornet* and *Yorktown* prepared to repel a major Japanese attack as the four aircraft carriers of the IJN's Combined Fleet neared the island.

In April the US Navy carrier fighter squadrons based in Hawaii had begun to convert to the F4F-4. The Coral Sea battle had shown the need for more fighters on carriers. Fortunately, the F4F-4's folding wings enabled the carrier fighter squadrons to increase their complement to 27 airplanes. The three US Navy fighter squadrons that saw action during the Midway battle – VF-3 aboard *Yorktown*, VF-6 aboard *Enterprise* and VF-8 aboard *Hornet* – all had F4F-4 Wildcats. Toward the end of May, VMF-221 (the sole US Marine Corps fighter squadron on Midway) received seven F4F-3 Wildcats to augment its 21 F2A-3s.

The flightdeck of *Hornet* on June 4, 1942, with the F4F-4 Wildcats of VF-8 warming up. (National Museum of Naval Aviation)

During the Japanese attack on Midway on the morning of June 4, 1942, future ace Capt Marion Carl shot down his first Zero-sen whilst flying a Wildcat. A short while later the American aircraft carriers sent off their strike groups to hit their Japanese counterparts. On board *Yorktown*, Lt Cdr John Thach made preparations to escort the TBD torpedo-bombers of VT-3. At the last minute, the eight VF-3 Wildcats he intended to take were cut to six. Thach instructed Machinist Tom Cheek to fly with his wingman, Ens Daniel Sheedy, as close escort to the TBDs, while Thach flew several thousand feet above with his division of four Wildcats as high escort. Thach had not had time to brief the two pilots (transferred in from VF-42) flying in his second section in his Beam Defense tactics.

Heading off, Cheek and Sheedy took station 1,000ft above the TBDs, while Thach and his division flew 3,000ft above. At 1003hrs one of the TBD crews spotted the Japanese carriers to the northwest and turned towards them. As the TBD formation and its six Wildcat escorts closed on the Japanese ships, a combat air patrol of some 40 Zero-sens fell on them.

Cheek watched as a fighter made a head-on run against the TBDs, then climbed up and around for another pass. "I was momentarily spellbound watching the fighter's clean, seemingly effortless maneuvers," he recalled. "Within seconds it was in a position to make a run on the last airplane on the formation's right flank. Nosing down slightly, the pilot continued his curving approach, 500ft above and slightly to my right, as though I had not yet been seen. I moved my engine controls into combat power range and pushed the throttle to the forward stop. Easing back on the control stick until the F4F was hanging on the prop, I brought the gunsight pip to an almost full deflection lead on the Zero's nose.

Lt Cdr John "Jimmy" Thach, second from right, with his pilots from VF-3, shortly before the Midway battle. Machinist Tom Cheek, on the left claimed a Zero-sen destroyed at Midway. (Courtesy Linda Cheek Hall)

"The six 0.50in. wing guns rumbled. I held the trigger down just long enough to see the red stream of tracers converge on the Zero's engine and start to drift back into the fuselage. The fighter's nose bucked momentarily, dropped back and then the airplane came diving down in my direction. At the moment my guns were still firing and the tracers were curving up and into their target, I was literally hanging in the air. The muzzle blast and recoil of the six 'fifties' was all that was needed to push my overloaded, underpowered, F4F over the edge into a control-sloppy stall. As I let my fighter's nose drop and started a recovery by rolling to the left, the Zero swept past on my right with black smoke and flames spewing from the engine, a river of fire trailing back along its belly."

The Zero-sens also fell on Thach's division flying above the TBDs, quickly hitting the F4F of the second section leader, Lt(jg) Brainard Macomber, knocking out his radio. They also shot down his wingman, Ens Edgar Bassett. Thrown on the defensive, Thach led his men in a series of maneuvers aimed at fending off the constant attacks by the Zero-sens. He also got a good burst off at an enemy fighter from close range as it pulled out of its attack.

Unable to raise Macomber on the radio, Thach ordered his wingman, Ens Robert "Ram" Dibb, whom he had trained in the Beam Defense, to pull away and act as a section leader. With Macomber sticking close on his wing and Dibb flying several hundred yards away, Thach started weaving, keeping a sharp lookout for Zero-sens. Soon enough one came in on Dibb, who radioed Thach that he had a fighter on his tail. Thach told Dibb to turn left into him, as they had practiced. Thach turned into Dibb for a head-on run against the Zero-sen attacking him. Coming under the fighter,

One of the pivotal events in the development of US Navy fighter tactics in World War II took place on June 4, 1942 during the Battle of Midway. That morning, Lt Cdr John Thach, commanding VF-3 embarked in *Yorktown*, took off with five other F4F-4s as escort to VT-3's TBD Devastators on their way to attack the Japanese carrier force. Approaching their targets, the formation ran into the Zero-sen combat air patrol, which immediately dove to attack the US Navy formation, shooting down one Wildcat from Thach's division of four. Thrown onto the defensive, Thach led his two remaining Wildcats in a series of evasive maneuvers as the Zero-sens swarmed around them. He decided to try out the Beam Defense tactic he had worked out before the war began and that he and his wingman, Ens Robert "Ram" Dibb, had practiced. Sending Dibb out to his right, and with Lt Brainard Macomber clinging closely onto his wing, Thach waited for his opportunity. As Thach recalled years later, "I got a shot at one or two of them and burned them. One of them had made a pass at my wingman, pulled out to the right and then came back. We were weaving continuously, and I got a head-on shot at him. Just about the time I saw this guy coming, 'Ram' had said 'There's a Zero on my tail'. He didn't have to look back because the Zero wasn't directly astern, but at about 45 degrees, beginning to follow him around. This gave me the head-on approach I desired. I was mad because, here, this poor little wingman who'd never been in combat before – in fact he had had very little gunnery training – and was experiencing his first time aboard a carrier, was about to have a Zero chew

Thach opened fire as the Zero-sen pulled up to pass over him. The Japanese fighter burst into flames as it went by. Thach's Beam Defense had worked exactly as he had intended. Under repeated attack, he and Dibb continued using the tactic, weaving and turning into the attacking Zero-sens as they came in on the Wildcats' tails. Thach shot down a third fighter, then stopped counting – Dibb claimed one as well.

VF-3 was the only Wildcat unit to engage the Zero-sens during the attack on the Japanese carriers, Thach and his fellow pilots claiming six fighters shot down and two more damaged. All but Bassett returned, with their Wildcats badly shot up. Later that day pilots from VF-3 tangled with Zero-sens during two attacks on *Yorktown*, claiming five shot down for the loss of four Wildcats. In many ways, however, the most important fighter battle of June 4 was Thach's successful debut of his Beam Defense during what the historian John Lundstrom has called "one of the classic encounters of the Pacific air war."

Despite the success of his new defensive tactic, Thach came out of the Midway fighting highly critical of the F4F-4. In his after action report he said, "It is indeed surprising that any of our pilots returned alive. Any success our fighter pilots may have had against the Japanese Zero fighter is <u>not</u> due to the performance of the airplane we fly but is the result of the comparatively poor marksmanship of the Japanese, stupid mistakes made by a few of their pilots and superior marksmanship and team work of some of our pilots. The F4F airplane is pitifully inferior in <u>climb</u>, <u>maneuverability</u> and <u>speed</u>."

GUADALCANAL

From the first landings on Guadalcanal on August 7, 1942 until the destruction of the last major Japanese convoy on the night of November 14/15 that ended the threat to the Island, US Marine Corps and US Navy Wildcat squadrons battled Zero-sen fighters. These aircraft were from the IJNAF's land- and carrier-based fighter units under the command of the Kichi Kūshū Butai (Base Air Force, administratively the 11th Kōkū Kantai (Air Fleet)) with its two component units, the 5th Kōkū Kūshū Butai (Air Attack Force) and the 6th Kōkū Kūshū Butai.

The mission of the Wildcat squadrons was to protect the vital airfields on Guadalcanal from the Japanese bombers attempting to destroy Henderson Field and the subsequently built Fighter 1 strip. Based at the former, the island's small force of SBD Dauntless dive-bombers and TBF Avenger torpedo-bombers of the 1st MAW, along with a handful of USAAF P-39 and P-400 Airacobras, were soon to be dubbed the "Cactus Air Force" after the code name for Guadalcanal. These airplanes regularly went out to attack enemy convoys bringing in supplies for the Japanese Army as it strived to take back the airfields from the Americans. The IJNAF urgently needed to establish air superiority over Guadalcanal to end the American air attacks on the convoys. With adequate men and supplies, the Japanese Army could then defeat US forces on the ground, retake the island and, it was hoped, exhaust the American will to continue fighting.

Establishing air superiority over the island was by no means a simple task. Guadalcanal lay 560 miles from Rabaul, the IJNAF's main base. For the Zero-sen pilots, this represented an exhausting six-hour flight to and from Guadalcanal – longer than the flight from Taiwan to Clark Field, in the Philippines, at the start of the war.

To make the flight to the island and then return to Rabaul, the Zero-sens had to be equipped with and retain their drop tanks. Even with the additional fuel, Japanese fighter pilots had only 15 minutes of flying time over Guadalcanal. And if damaged in combat, their only alternative was the long flight back to Rabaul.

The IJNAF had been surprisingly lackadaisical about building additional airfields at Rabaul, or in-between Rabaul and the islands along the Solomon chain to the south. From early August until early October, when the Japanese completed an airstrip at Buin, on the southeast coast of Bougainville, there were no airfields between Rabaul and Guadalcanal apart from a rough emergency field on Buka Island, northeast of Bougainville. This lack of facilities meant that the IJNAF could not deploy all the air units it had available, nor could it use the shorter range Type 0 Model 32 fighters as escorts for the Type 1 bombers for a full two months.

Not unlike their RAF counterparts during the Battle of Britain, the Wildcat squadrons on Guadalcanal had two advantages that proved critical during the air battles – an early warning system and proximity to their airfields. Before the war the Royal Australian Navy had established a network of observers along the Solomon Island chain equipped with radios. The Coastwatchers, as they were called, gave vital early warning of Japanese formations heading south to Guadalcanal. Alerted to an incoming raid, US Marine Corps radar stations on the island could pick up the Japanese formations when they were 125–140 miles away from the island. This gave the Wildcat squadrons the critical time they needed to get their slow-climbing fighters to higher altitude, above the Japanese bomber formations and in a position to intercept. As "Jimmy" Flatley had found, against the more maneuverable Zero-sen altitude was critical.

In the air battles that followed an interception, the Wildcat pilots would often break away from combat with the Zero-sens with their airplanes mangled and engines damaged. On numerous occasions Marine and Naval Aviators brought their aircraft back for a safe landing, while their Japanese opponents struggled, and often failed, to return safely to Rabaul.

The air battles began the day of the landings, US Navy Wildcats from VF-5 (USS *Saratoga* (CV-3)), VF-6 (*Enterprise*) and VF-71 (*Wasp*) covering troops as they came ashore on Tulagi and Guadalcanal on August 7. In the first contest between US Navy carrier fighters and a land-based IJNAF fighter group, the Wildcats received a mauling from the experienced aces of the Tainan Kokutai flying out of Rabaul – nine of eighteen Wildcats were shot down in fierce fighting.

On August 20 the first US Marine Corps fighter squadron arrived at Henderson Field when VMF-223 (from Marine Air Group (MAG) 23), with 19 F4F-4 Wildcats, flew in from USS *Long Island* (ACV-1).

OVERLEAF *continued*
him to pieces. I probably should have decided to duck under this Zero, but I lost my temper a little bit and I decided I'm going to keep my fire going into him and he's going to pull out, which he did. He just missed me by a few feet, and I saw flames coming out of the bottom of his airplane." Thach's maneuver worked as well as he had hoped. Dubbed the "Thach Weave" by Lt Cdr James Flatley, who successfully employed the tactic during the Battle of Santa Cruz, Thach's maneuver became the standard defensive counter employed by all US Navy and US Marine Corps fighter pilots when dealing with the Zero-sen's superior maneuverability.

Pilots of the crack Tainan Kokutai pose for a newspaper photographer at Rabaul in June 1942. Moments after this shot was taken an air raid alarm sounded and the pilots scurried off into action. (Maru)

Under the command of Maj John L. Smith, VMF-223 was staffed by a mix of experienced pilots, including Capt Marion Carl, and newly fledged fighter pilots fresh from training. VMF-224, under Maj Robert Galer, arrived as reinforcements on August 30. Shortly after, following damage to *Saratoga*, Lt Cdr Leroy Simpler brought VF-5 ashore to Henderson Field for a spell of operations. With replacement pilots drawn from other US Marine Corps squadrons in the South Pacific, these three units bore the brunt of the air fighting until mid-October.

The day after their arrival, the pilots of VMF-223 had their first run-in with Zero-sens when Smith and his division engaged six Japanese fighters while on patrol. He claimed one shot down when his attacker pulled up directly in front of him, but the Zero-sens shot up all four Wildcats, forcing one pilot to make the first of many Wildcat dead-stick landings at Henderson Field. The encounter gave Smith and his pilots confidence in the F4F's rugged construction.

On August 24, during the Battle of the Eastern Solomons, VMF-223 intercepted a strike force of Type 97 Carrier Attack airplanes with a Zero-sen escort from the light carrier *Ryūjō* that had been sent to attack Guadalcanal. The American pilots claimed 11 bombers and five Zero-sens destroyed for the loss of three Wildcats (in fact the IJNAF had lost three bombers and one Zero-sen, and claimed 15 Wildcats shot down in return). Capt Marion Carl claimed three bombers and one Zero-sen, making him the first US Marine Corps ace. In the carrier battle fought that same day US Navy airplanes sank *Ryūjō* and Wildcat pilots from VF-5 and VF-6 claimed 15 Zero-sens shot down. Ens Francis Register of VF-6, who would subsequently become the only US Navy pilot to claim five Zero-sens destroyed during 1942, downed two of the fighters to open his score against the A6M.

Forty-eight hours later the 5th Kōkū Kūshū Butai launched the first of many bombing raids against Guadalcanal, sending

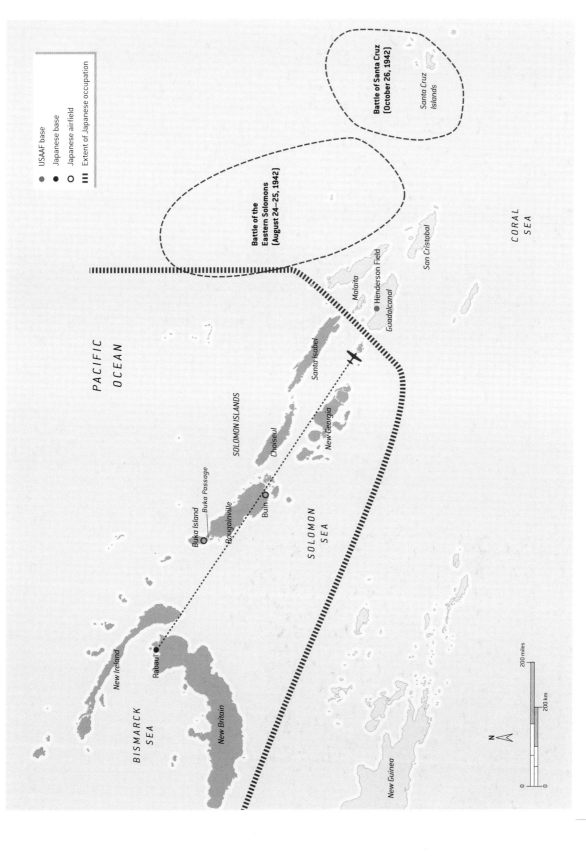

USAAF base
Japanese base
Japanese airfield
Extent of Japanese occupation

Battle of Santa Cruz
(October 26, 1942)

Santa Cruz
Islands

Battle of the
Eastern Solomons
(August 24–25, 1942)

PACIFIC
OCEAN

CORAL
SEA

Malaita
Henderson Field
Guadalcanal
San Cristobal

Santa Isabel

SOLOMON ISLANDS

Choiseul

New Georgia

Buka Passage

Buka Island

Bougainville

Buin

SOLOMON
SEA

BISMARCK
SEA

New Ireland

Rabaul

New Britain

New Guinea

N

200 miles

200 km

0

0

Capt Marion Carl, from VMF-223, claimed a total of 16.5 kills over Guadalcanal during 1942. Eight of his victories were Zero-sens. (80G-357168, RG 80, NARA)

out 16 Type 1 Attack Bombers ("Betty") from the 4th Kokutai with an escort of Zero-sen fighters from the Tainan Kokutai. As the bombers came over Henderson Field in an impressive V-formation, Smith led three divisions in to intercept them – the VMF-223 pilots duly claimed eight bombers and five Zero-sens destroyed. In reality three Japanese fighters had been lost that day, one of which was flown by Lt(jg) Junichi Sasai, the top-scoring Tainan Kokutai pilot at Rabaul. Marion Carl had claimed a Zero-sen destroyed in a high-side run and then had a second A6M jump him as he came in to land at Henderson. In a head-on run, Carl held his fire until the Zero-sen pulled up in front of him, at which point the fighter exploded.

Four days later, on August 30, *Shōkaku* and *Zuikaku* sent out a fighter sweep to Guadalcanal. Smith was flying at 15,000ft with seven other Wildcats and seven P-400s from the 67th Fighter Squadron when they saw Zero-sens below them. Coming in out of the sun, the Wildcats claimed eight IJNAF fighters on their first pass, before using their speed to climb back up to altitude for a second run. In the space of three minutes the US Marine Corps pilots claimed 14 Zero-sens shot down for no loss. Smith was credited with four victories and Marion Carl three, this being their best day against the Mitsubishi fighter. The Japanese appear to have lost nine A6Ms, all flown by veteran carrier pilots.

Over the next two weeks, until bad weather over Rabaul brought a hiatus, the Japanese carried out eight raids on Guadalcanal. The units at Rabaul were all below their authorized strength, so the raids typically consisted of 18 or 27 Type 1 bombers, with an escort of 12 to 14 Zero-sens flying behind and above the bomber formation.

John Smith quickly developed intercept tactics that all subsequent US Marine Corps and US Navy Wildcat squadrons fighting on Guadalcanal adopted. When they had adequate warning, Smith would lead his divisions up to an altitude some 4,000–5,000ft above the Japanese bomber formation, pulling ahead and off to one side of the enemy airplanes. The Wildcats would then take the opposite course, flying toward the bombers and then rolling in on a high-side run to avoid the Type 1's 20mm tail gun. If they could, the Wildcat pilots launched

An F4F-4 lands on Guadalcanal. Rough field conditions such as those seen here resulted in a high number of operational losses during this campaign. (National Museum of Naval Aviation)

their attack from right to left in sections, pulling up in a climbing turn to the left after their first pass to take stock. If there were no Zero-sens around, they would carry out another attack on the bombers.

When the escorts did attempt to intercept them, the Wildcat pilots would try for a quick high-side pass and a deflection shot before diving away, using their speed and rapid maneuvering to escape the Zero-sens if they could. Maneuvering combat, in which the IJNAF fighter excelled, was to be avoided. US Marine Corps and US Navy pilots found that when the Zero-sens bounced them they would often overshoot and recover ahead of the Wildcat, leaving themselves open for a devastating burst of 0.50in. fire.

Flying behind the bomber formations, the Zero-sen pilots had difficulty countering the American hit-and-run tactics. When they did catch the Wildcats, they were astonished at the Grumman fighter's ability to absorb punishing fire, compared with their lighter Zero-sens. It seemed to some that the 7.7mm rounds would barely penetrate the wings of a Wildcat. In his memoir, Saburo Sakai recorded his amazement when, in his one combat with a Wildcat, he fired more than 200 rounds of 7.7mm ammunition into his opponent. The Zero-sen ace noted that "the Wildcat continued flying as if nothing had happened."

The 20mm cannon was also proving less than ideal in combat with a wildly maneuvering Wildcat because of its low rate-of-fire. This meant that getting a sufficient number of shells into an F4F to bring it down was a challenge for all but the best marksmen. As one US Marine Corps officer put it, with some exaggeration, "a Zero can't take two seconds' fire from a Grumman, and a Grumman can sometimes take as high as 15 minutes fire from a Zero."

Lt(jg) Junichi Sasai was the top-scoring Tainan Kokutai pilot at Rabaul at the time of his death in combat with VMF-223 on August 26, 1942. Having first seen action during the invasion of the Philippines in December 1941, he had claimed 54 victories prior to being killed. A veteran of 76 missions with the Tainan Kokutai, Sasai was officially credited with 27 kills. (S. Sakai)

The American pilots impressed and surprised at least some of their opponents with their tactics and their aggressiveness. Long after the war had ended, one Zero-sen pilot who fought over Guadalcanal recalled that "behind the thick glass [of their canopies] the enemy pilots were surprisingly young, dignified-looking. And although they were young, they were highly skilled and well trained. They escaped us quickly" . . . but not always. On September 9 the US Marine Corps lost three Wildcats to the Zero-sens. Four days later three more US Marine Corps F4Fs were downed, as were two US Navy examples.

Maj John Smith was the CO of VMF-223 when it became the first fighter squadron to be based on Guadalcanal. He quickly devised successful tactics for intercepting Japanese bombers following his unit's arrival at Henderson Field. (80G-20665, RG 80, NARA)

Legendary ace CPO Saburo Sakai engaged the Wildcat only once, on August 7, 1942. Participating in the first long-range mission flown by Zero-sens to Guadalcanal, he shot down the F4F-4 flown by future ace Lt J. J. Southerland of VF-5. Minutes later he downed a lone SBD from VS-71, only to then be severely wounded by return fire from eight Dauntlesses from VB-6 that he had attempted to intercept – Sakai had mistaken them for Wildcats. Despite having suffered terrible head wounds that left him almost totally blind (he eventually lost the sight in his right eye), Sakai somehow managed to fly back to Rabaul. (S. Sakai)

After a two-week weather-related lull, the Japanese resumed their attacks with a change in escort tactics. A reinforced 5th Kōkū Kūshū Butai increased the number of escorting Zero-sens and divided the fighters into two forces – the direct escort force covering the bombers from behind and an air control force sweeping ahead of the bomber formation to disrupt the enemy fighters as they climbed to intercept.

On September 27 the new tactic was tried out for the first time, but it failed. The air control force saw no American fighters and headed back to Rabaul. The bombers saw the Wildcats rising up to meet them, but as the Zero-sens had no radios, they had no way of contacting their escort. Two bombers were lost over Guadalcanal and one on the way back to base. The next day things were even worse. Wildcats from VMF-223, VMF-224 and VF-5 shot down five Type 1 bombers, two more crash landed and one was scrapped – a 30 percent loss rate for the mission. Increasing the size of the escort had failed to protect the bombers, so the 5th Kōkū Kūshū Butai decided on a new tactic – using the bombers as a feint to draw up the Wildcats for a Zero-sen fighter sweep.

The first attempt at this tactic, on September 29, brought mixed success, but on October 2 the Zero-sen pilots scored their most decisive victory over US Marine Corps and US Navy Wildcats in a near perfect ambush. Maj Smith scrambled with 13 Wildcats from VMF-223 and VMF-224. Climbing out of the clouds at 25,000ft, he was shocked to see 17 Zero-sens diving down on his division. The IJNAF fighters shot up Smith's Wildcat, forcing him to crash land a few miles from the airfield. Fellow ace Maj Robert Galer was shot down, for the second time, and three other US Marine Corps and one VF-5 pilot were missing.

Having recognized the change in tactics, Marine and Naval Aviators turned the tables on their Zero-sen attackers the very next day. Heading towards Guadalcanal, 27 IJNAF fighter pilots found extensive cloud cover, so they split the formation up into three separate Chutai. Having been alerted to the approaching enemy airplanes, 29 Wildcats

An F4F-4 damaged on Guadalcanal in one of the many Japanese air raids on the island. Aircraft such as this became a valuable source of spare parts for those still operational. (127GW-8791-61572, RG 127, NARA)

from VMF-223, VMF-224 and VF-5 took off and climbed higher than usual. Flying at 33,000ft, Capt Marion Carl, with four other Wildcat pilots, looked down to see Zero-sens flying well below him in a broad V-formation. Diving down, Carl came in on the last fighter on the right, opening fire from 100 yards and seeing the Zero-sen burst into flame. Within a few minutes Carl's division had shot down five fighters.

Lt Col Joseph Bauer, CO of VMF-212 and an experienced and aggressive fighter pilot, was flying with Carl's division that day, and he claimed four Zero-sens shot down. Carl's division claimed nine fighters in total (for once this figure was close to the number of Zero-sens actually lost) at a cost of one Wildcat – one of the best scores achieved by either side during the entire campaign.

Type 0 Model 21 fighters preparing to take off for a mission to Guadalcanal. The Japanese also suffered operational losses from poor field conditions and inadequate maintenance. (Author's collection)

On October 9, 1942, VMF-121 from MAG-14 arrived on Guadalcanal, followed shortly thereafter by Bauer's VMF-212, to replace the battered VMF-223 and VMF-224, whose exhausted survivors departed three days later. VMF-121's executive officer, Capt Joseph Foss, began his astonishing run against the Zero-sen on October 13. On the voyage across the Pacific, Foss and his squadronmates had studied "Jimmy" Flatley's manual on fighter tactics. Foss clearly took its lessons to heart. Over the next 12 days he would claim 15 Zero-sens shot down to become the leading scorer against the Mitsubishi fighter in 1942.

Foss' first victory was almost his last. Going after a group of Zero-sens escorting "Betty" bombers, Foss failed to spot a fighter behind him. However, his opponent made the mistake of overshooting the inattentive Foss, who quickly fired at the Zero-sen and claimed it destroyed. Moments later the remaining IJNAF fighters in the attacking shotai badly damaged his Wildcat when they followed him all the way back to Fighter 1, where Foss made a barely controlled landing. Learning quickly from experience, he downed another Zero-sen the next day. In his autobiography Foss recalled that "experience put the finishing touches on my fighter training. I quickly learned that the best results came when I flew close to a Zero before opening fire. I always tried to surprise the enemy by coming up on his tail, but if I ended up playing a game of chicken with him, I would wait until the Zero pulled up to avoid a collision and then I'd send a short burst into the base of his wing."

Lt Col Joe Bauer was appointed head of Cactus Fighter Command on October 17. The aggressive Bauer told his pilots to challenge the Zero-sens in head-on runs, relying on the Wildcat's armament to knock them down. "When you see Zeros", Bauer said, "dogfight'em!" The Kichi Kōkū Butai gave the Marine and Naval Aviators plenty of opportunity to do so, launching a seven-day campaign timed to coincide with a ground offensive that was intended to overcome the US Marine Corps and US Army defenders once and for all.

A Type 0 Model 21 fighter accelerates down the flightdeck of an IJN carrier during the Battle of Santa Cruz, which was fought on October 25–27, 1942. (P02887_001, Australian War Memorial)

Taking Bauer's admonition to heart, Joe Foss claimed two Zero-sens at the very beginning of the offensive on October 18, adding two more two days later, four on October 23 and a remarkable five in two missions 48 hours later. Between October 18–23, the US Marine Corps and US Navy Wildcat pilots actually shot down 12 Zero-sens (although they claimed 50!) for the loss of seven F4Fs. On October 25 – the last day of the offensive – the Japanese sent out wave after wave of fighters and bombers against Guadalcanal, losing 11 Zero-sens to the 1st MAW, which had two Wildcats destroyed in return. This steady attrition was robbing the IJNAF's fighter kokutai of many of their best pilots.

The next day saw the final carrier clash of 1942, the Battle of Santa Cruz, which resulted in a tactical defeat for the US Navy with the loss of *Hornet* and damage to *Enterprise*. Fighter losses were about even. In attacks on the Japanese carriers and defense of their own task force, 13 Wildcats were shot down and another ten ditched or crashed, while the Japanese carriers had 15 Zero-sens shot down and another nine lost to ditching or other crashes.

Lt Cdr "Jimmy" Flatley, commanding VF-10 aboard *Enterprise*, had learned Thach's Beam Defense tactic from Lt Butch O'Hare over the summer, and he duly trained his pilots in the technique. Escorting VT-10's torpedo-bombers in an attack on the Japanese carriers, several of Flatley's pilots utilized the Beam Defense when they came under attack. Leading a division in defense of Task Force 16 that afternoon,

Deck crews unfold the wings of an F4F-4 from VF-10 on board *Enterprise* during the Battle of Santa Cruz. (80G-30005, RG 80, NARA)

Flatley employed the Beam Defense against attacking Zero-sens and became a convert. He dubbed the maneuver the "Thach Weave" and did much to promote it. The "Thach Weave" became the standard US Marine Corps and US Navy defensive and escort tactic against the Zero-sen for the rest of the Pacific War.

After a comparative lull, the Japanese made one final push to retake Guadalcanal in mid-November 1942, assembling a convoy of 12 transports with formidable naval escort. Both sides had reinforced their air units, the Kichi Kōkū Butai gaining the 1st Kōkū Kūshū Butai (with one Type 1 bomber group and three Zero-sen groups) to replace the battered 5th Kōkū Kūshū Butai, which returned to Japan. The 1st MAW added more Wildcats from VMF-121, VMF-212 and VMO-251, while the USAAF flew in more P-39s and new P-38 Lightnings.

On November 11 the Japanese sent out two raids. The Wildcats failed to find Type 99 Carrier Bombers in the clouds around the island, but the Zero-sen escort jumped a flight of six F4Fs, shooting down four pilots for the loss of two fighters. Later that morning the Wildcats shot down four Type 1 bombers. The next day the 6th Kōkū Kūshū Butai sortied 16 Type 1 bombers armed with torpedoes, with an escort of 30 Zero-sens, to attack American transports off Guadalcanal. The intercepting

Lt Hideki Shingo departs the carrier *Shōkaku* on October 26, 1942 as part of the second-wave attack on the US Task Force during the Battle of Santa Cruz – pilots in this wave claimed five enemy aircraft shot down. Shingo was the squadron leader of the vessel's embarked Zero-sen fighter force, having previously seen combat in China and the early months of the Pacific War. (via Aerospace Publishing)

Wildcats and P-39s destroyed 11 of the bombers, and the remaining five were written off due to battle damage. On November 13–14 there were intensive air battles over the convoy the IJN was trying to get to Guadalcanal. US Marine Corps Wildcat pilots claimed 21 Zero-sens shot down, while Flatley's VF-10, flown in to Guadalcanal, was credited with eight A6Ms destroyed on the 14th.

The destruction of the convoy and the loss of IJN warships attempting to protect the merchant vessels in the Battle of Guadalcanal ended the Japanese effort to retake the island.

The last confrontation between the Wildcat and the Zero-sen in 1942 took place just before Christmas over Munda Point, on the island of New Georgia, where the Japanese were belatedly building an airfield closer to Guadalcanal. On December 23, Maj Donald Yost of VMF-121, escorting US Marine Corps SBDs that had been sent to bomb the new airfield, claimed two Zero-sens shot down. He enjoyed even more success on a similar mission the next day when he intercepted six A6Ms and claimed four destroyed.

Years later Yost recalled how he missed the Zero-sens on his first pass on December 24, but spotted a weak point in their tactics as they flew by him. For some reason, as each fighter went past him, its pilot recovered by doing a slow roll. Years later, as Yost

F4F-4 Wildcats on Fighter 1 around the time of the final battles on Guadalcanal in mid-November 1942. A formation of B-17s flies overhead. (127 GW-879H-52620, RG 127, NARA)

recalled, "I anticipated where he would be in his roll. I was shooting at him before he got on his back. When he got there, he was a ball of fire." Aside from his four Zero-sens destroyed, Yost's wingman, Lt Kenneth Kirk Jr from VMO-251, claimed three.

The one-sided result from this final aerial engagement of the year was a measure of how far US Marine Corps and US Navy pilots had progressed in their battles with the Zero-sen, and evidence of the beginning of the inexorable decline in the quality of the IJNAF.

The first F4F-3 Wildcats were fitted with a telescopic gunsight extending through the windscreen. Although more accurate than the older ring and bead sights of the 1930s, the telescopic sight sharply restricted the pilot's field of vision at a critical point in air combat. During 1941 the US Navy introduced illuminated reflector gunsights, initially borrowing the USAAC's N2 sight while working on its own design. When the latter proved problematic, the US Navy obtained copies of the RAF's Barr & Stroud Mk II Reflector Sight and arranged for production in the USA as the Illuminated Sight Mk 8. Much more effective for deflection shooting, the Mk 8 was fitted to the F4F-4 after the Battle of Midway.

Gunnery training for fighter pilots drummed in the two most critical questions — where to aim, and when to fire.

Naval Aviators were taught how to calculate the correct lead, or deflection, using the Mk 8 sight until it became automatic, and to open fire when no more than 1,000ft away from their target. The Wildcat's guns were set to converge at 1,000ft and closer. Many found that against the Zero-sen it paid to get in even closer, and to fire when only a few hundred feet away.

Most importantly, pilots had to learn to calculate the proper deflection, and determine the range almost instantly. Capt Marion Carl later wrote:

"I was blessed with the ability to look at another airplane and instantly know what it could do relative to my speed and position. I rarely made conscious decisions in a combat — mostly, I acted on instinct."

STATISTICS AND ANALYSIS

In the carrier battles at Coral Sea and Midway, and in the nearly three months of intensive air combat around Guadalcanal that followed, US Marine Corps and US Navy Wildcat pilots flying an airplane that was in many ways inferior to the Zero-sen did well in air combat against their adversary, and held their own against the best IJNAF fighter pilots.

In the ferocity of combat both sides over-claimed the number of airplanes they had shot down (the Japanese to a far greater extent than the Americans) – by no means an uncommon occurrence during World War II. The actual loss figures show that the Wildcat pilots did surprisingly well. John Lundstrom found that at Coral Sea and Midway the US Navy's Wildcat squadrons actually shot down 14 Zero-sens for the loss of ten F4Fs. During the most intensive period of action in the skies over Guadalcanal, from August 7 through to November 15, 1942, research by Lundstrom, James Sawruk and Richard Frank indicates that the fighter units of the Kichi Kōkū Butai lost 72 Zero-sens in aerial combat while the 1st MAW had 70 Wildcats destroyed. Finally, the Japanese carrier air groups lost 43 Zero-sens in aerial combat, the majority of these almost certainly falling to carrier-based Wildcat squadrons, who in turn lost 31 Wildcats. This gives a total of 129 Zero-sens lost from May to November 1942 against the loss of 111 Wildcats.

What is more significant is what lies behind these numbers. From one perspective, the US Navy's carrier force fought the IJN's Combined Fleet to a draw – both sides lost four fleet carriers during 1942. But this was in reality a victory for the United States, as it sharply reduced Japanese offensive power and inflicted losses that the US Navy, supported by a far greater industrial capacity, could more easily replace.

Capt Joseph Foss, the highest scoring Wildcat pilot against the Zero-sen, with the other members of his VMF-121 flight. They are, from left to right, Roger Habermann, Danny Doyle, Foss, Bill Marontate and Roy Ruddell. Doyle and Ruddell were both killed in combat. (National Museum of Naval Aviation)

In the carrier battles of the Coral Sea, Midway, the Eastern Solomons and Santa Cruz, the IJNAF suffered irreplaceable losses among its elite pilots. During the air battles over Guadalcanal no fewer than 95 Type 1 bombers were destroyed and most of their crews killed – many of the best Zero-sen pilots perished trying to defend these aircraft. The famous Tainan Kokutai, for example, lost 32 pilots fighting over Guadalcanal. These men, too, particularly the Chutai and Shotai leaders, were irreplaceable.

The US Marine Corps and US Navy Wildcat pilots on Guadalcanal, who did the bulk of the air fighting in defense of the island, prevented the Japanese from establishing air superiority. Had they failed, Guadalcanal might well have been retaken. While the fighting on the island continued until the Japanese evacuation in February 1943, it was the Japanese who were exhausted, not the Americans.

Three factors contributed to the success of the Wildcat against the Zero-sen – its structural strength and protection for fuel and pilot, better armament and gunnery, and tactics. When reading accounts of the air battles in the Pacific War from this period, one encounters time and again stories of Wildcats coming back with shredded tails, wings full of holes, shattered cockpits and instrument panels, and engines damaged, but still returning to a carrier deck or one of the airfields on Guadalcanal. Lacking armor protection for the pilot and self-sealing fuel tanks, the Zero-sen simply could not stand up to such punishment. Where Wildcat pilots survived, Zero-sen pilots, more often than not, died. It is interesting to note that all three of the top US Marine Corps aces against the Zero-sen at Guadalcanal – Marion Carl, Joe Foss and John Smith – were shot down but survived to fight again.

Pilots from the Tainan Kokutai's 2nd Squadron come together for a group photograph at Rabaul on the eve of the Guadalcanal campaign. In the front row, from left to right, are PO3/cs Yoshizo Ohashi, Seiji Ishikawa (5 victories) and Kenichi Kumagai (2 victories), Seaman 1/c Kenichiro Yamamoto and PO2/c Shin Nakano. In the second row, from left to right, are PO2/c Toshio Ota (34 victories), PO1/c Saburo Sakai (60+ victories), Seaman 1/c Masayoshi Yonekawa (6 victories) and PO/3c Unichi Miya. Standing, from left to right, are PO1/c Hiroyoshi Nishizawa (86 victories), PO3/cs Daizo Fukumori, Yutaka Kimura and Masuaki Endo (14 victories), PO1/c Katsumi Kobayashi and PO3/c Takeichi Kokubu. Of this group, only Sakai and Ishikawa survived the war. (via Henry Sakaida)

While many Naval Aviators criticized the reduction in ammunition that came with the increase to six 0.50in. machine guns in the F4F-4, a burst of fire, especially at close range, was devastating against the Zero-sen's unprotected fuel tanks. While the A6M's 20mm cartridge was heavier and individually more destructive than a 0.50in. shell, the weight of fire of a two-second burst from the Zero-sen's two 20mm cannon was actually less than a two-second burst from the six faster-firing 0.50in. machine guns installed in the wings of the Wildcat.

The US Navy's emphasis on deflection shooting was critical to the success of many Wildcat pilots. Trying to get on the tail of a Zero-sen risked getting involved in a slower-speed turning fight where the Japanese machine held the advantage. US Marine Corps and US Navy Wildcat pilots learned to take snap shots from all angles. Having guns of the same caliber also gave them an advantage in deflection shooting over their Japanese counterparts. The Zero-sen's mixed armament of 7.7mm machine guns and 20mm cannon, with different muzzle velocities and rates of fire, made deflection shooting more complicated.

Tactics were also critical to the Wildcat's success. Men like James Flatley, John Thach and John Smith (all experienced fighter pilots) developed tactics to negate the Zero-sen's phenomenal maneuverability and enable the Wildcat pilots to use their superior armament and training in deflection shooting to get in a killing blow. The hit-and-run attack, a quick burst and then a high-speed twisting dive away from the target proved effective, as did the Thach Weave as a defensive tactic. With the Zero-sen being unable to match the F4F in a dive, and suffering reduced aileron response at higher speeds, IJNAF pilots found these tactics difficult to counter.

The tactics the Wildcat pilots developed during 1942, and the lessons they learned, became standard for Naval Aviators for the rest of the Pacific War.

VMF-121's Capt Joseph Foss emerged as the highest-scoring US Marine Corps or US Navy pilot against the Zero-sen during the Guadalcanal campaign with 16 victory claims – he added three more A6Ms to his total on January 15, 1943 for his final kills of the Pacific War. Maj John Smith and Capt Marion Carl, both from VMF-223, were credited with eight victories against the Zero-sen over Guadalcanal.

Of the 12 US Marine Corps and US Navy Wildcat pilots who claimed five or more Zero-sen victories during 1942, half had completed their flying training before June 1941 and half after that date. That the former should have done well in air combat is less of a surprise given their greater flying experience, and the fact that most were leading squadrons or divisions in combat. That several younger pilots only a few months out of training claimed almost as many victories is a tribute not only to their flying ability, but to the US Navy's training program and good tactics.

Regrettably, although a number of IJNAF aces fought during the Guadalcanal campaign, Japanese records do not note their individual victories.

Leading A6M Type 0 Killers in 1942			
Ace	Unit(s)	Zero-sen Claims	Total Claims
Capt Joseph Foss	VMF-121	16	26
Maj John Smith	VMF-223	8	19
Capt Marion Carl	VMF-223	8	18.5
Maj Robert Galer	VMF-224	6	13
Lt Col Harold Bauer	VMF-212	6	11
Lt Jack Conger	VMF-223/212	6	10
Maj Donald Yost	VMF-121	6	8
2Lt Cecil Doyle	VMF-121	5	5
2Lt Kenneth Frazer	VMF-223	5	12.5
Lt James Percy	VMF-112	5	6
Capt Francis Pierce	VMF-121	5	6
Ens Francis Register	VF-6/5	5	7
Capt Loren Everton	VMF-212	4	10
Mar Gun Henry Hamilton	VMF-223/212	4	7
2Lt Roger Haberman	VMF-121	3.5	6.5
2Lt Joseph Narr	VMF-121	3	7
2Lt William Freeman	VMF-121	3	6
2Lt Kenneth Pond	VMF-223	3	6
Lt Cdr John Thach	VF-3	3	6
Lt(jg) Scott McCusky	VF-42/3	3	13.5

AFTERMATH

On February 12, 1943, the first F4U-1 Corsairs arrived on Guadalcanal with VMF-124. As the months went by, the Corsair progressively replaced the Wildcat in US Marine Corps' land-based fighter squadrons in the South Pacific. By August all eight such units were flying the Corsair. The US Navy's Wildcat squadrons continued battling the Zero-sens over the Solomons until the end of the summer of 1943. By then the superior Grumman F6F Hellcat had begun to replace the Wildcat aboard the Pacific Fleet's new *Essex*-class fleet carriers and *Independence*-class light carriers. As the US Navy's principal carrier fighter for the remainder of the Pacific War, the Hellcat would establish a dominance over the Zero-sen using the tactics the Wildcat pilots had pioneered during 1942.

Newly arrived F4U-1 Corsairs of VMF-124 in February 1943. The Japanese viewed the Vought fighter as the first American airplane that could seriously challenge the Zero-sen. (80G-41100, RG 80, NARA)

The F4F gained a new lease on life as a fighter flying from the many small escort carriers built to provide close air support to the amphibious landings in the Pacific. The Eastern Aircraft Division built 4,437 FM-2 Wildcats for the US Navy. With a more powerful engine, lighter weight, and with armament reduced to four 0.50in. machine guns, the FM-2 offered drastically improved performance over the F4F-4. During the invasions of the Philippines and Okinawa, FM-2s established a kill ratio of 32-to-1, admittedly against older types of Japanese aircraft and less well-trained pilots. This figure was remarkable nonetheless.

The Zero-sen was destined to soldier on until the very end of the Pacific War. With the introduction of the Corsair and the Hellcat, as well as the second generation of USAAF fighters (P-38, P-47 and P-51), the Zero-sen lost its ascendancy and never regained it. Modest improvements incorporated into the A6M5 Type 0 Carrier Fighter Model 52 gave increases in maximum and diving speeds and improved armament, but at a cost to maneuverability, and still left the Zero-sen well short of its American adversaries in terms of performance.

The prototype FM-2 Wildcat, built by the Eastern Aircraft Division of the General Motors Corporation. (80G-224669, RG 80, NARA)

As the training of IJNAF fighter pilots declined steadily as the conflict progressed, few could get the best out of their airplanes. However, in the hands of the few remaining veterans, the Zero-sen could still be a deadly adversary. Indeed, Corsair and Hellcat pilots could never completely ignore the admonition "Never dogfight with a Zero." Towards the end of the Pacific War Zero-sen pilots were going into combat with 200 flying hours or less – perhaps a quarter of what their opponents had.

A captured Mitsubishi A6M5 Type 0 Carrier Fighter Model 52 is put through its paces near war's end. With no real replacement, the Zero-sen soldiered on until the very end of the fighting in the Pacific. (80G-248975, RG 80, NARA)

The Zero-sen's intended replacement, the Mitsubishi A7M Reppu, encountered innumerable delays in its development and never entered production. Two fighters that might have helped address the balance, the Mitsubishi J2M Raiden and the Kawanishi N1K2-J Shiden Kai, were built in too few numbers. The IJNAF had no choice but to continue with the Zero-sen as its main fighter, Mitsubishi and Nakajima completing construction of 10,449 examples before war's end. Many were destroyed as kamikaze, with poorly trained pilots heading off to die attacking the American fleet off Okinawa.

FURTHER READING

Aviation History Unit, *The Navy's Air War – Mission Completed* (Harper Brothers, 1946)

Carl, Maj Gen Marion E. USMC (Ret) with Barrett Tillman, *Pushing the Envelope – The Career of Fighter Ace and Test Pilot Marion Carl* (Naval Institute Press, 1994)

Ewing, Steve, *Reaper Leader – The Life of "Jimmy" Flatley* (Naval Institute Press, 2002)

Ewing, Steve, *Thach Weave – The Life of "Jimmy" Thach* (Naval Institute Press, 2004)

Foss, Joe and Donna Wild Foss, *A Proud American – The Autobiography of Joe Foss* (Pocket Books, 1992)

Frank, Richard, *Guadalcanal* (Random House, 1990)

Greene, Frank L., *History of the Grumman F4F Wildcat* (Grumman Aircraft Engineering Corporation)

Hata, Ikuhiko, Yasuho Izawa and Christopher Shores, *Japanese Naval Air Force Fighter Units and Their Aces 1932–1945* (Grub Street, 2011)

Horikoshi, Jiro, *Eagles of Mitsubishi – The Story of the Zero Fighter* (University of Washington Press, 1981)

Lundstrom, John B., *The First Team – Pacific Naval Air Combat from Pearl Harbor to Midway* (Naval Institute Press, 1984)

Lundstrom, John B., *The First Team and the Guadalcanal Campaign – Naval Fighter Combat from August to November 1942* (Naval Institute Press, 1994)

Mikesh, Robert C., *Zero – Combat and Development History of Japan's Legendary Mitsubishi A6M Zero Fighter* (Motorbooks International, 1994)

Miller, Thomas G. Jr., *The Cactus Air Force – The Story of the Handful of Fliers Who Saved Guadalcanal* (Harper and Row, 1969)

Minora, Akimoto, *Reisen Ku Senki – Vol. 1: Reisen no Eiko* (Chronicle of the Reisen Battles: Vol. 1 – Glory of the Reisen) (Kojinsha, 2010)

Minora, Akimoto, *Reisen Ku Senki – Vol. 3: Fukutsu no Reisen* (Chronicle of the Reisen Battles: Vol. 3 – The Invincible Reisen) (Kojinsha, 2010)

Okumiya, Masatake and Jiro Horikoshi with Martin Caidin, *The Zero Fighter* (Cassel & Co., 1958)

Peattie, Mark R., *Sunburst – The Rise of Japanese Naval Air Power, 1909–1941* (Naval Institute Press, 2001)

Sherrod, Robert, *History of Marine Corps Aviation in World War II* (Combat Forces Press, 1952)

Wilmott, H. P., *The War With Japan – The Period of Balance May 1942–October 1943* (SR Books, 2002)

Wilmott, H. P., *Empires in the Balance: Japanese and Allied Pacific Strategies to April 1942* (Naval Institute Press, 1982)

INDEX

References to illustrations are shown in **bold**.

20mm cannon, Oerlikon Type 99-1 12, 19, 22, 30, 31, 32-3, **33**, 34, 66, 67, 75

aerial gunnery 48, 48, **72**, 75
Aioi, Lt Takahide 20
Akagi (Japanese carrier) **22**, 39

Bassett, Ens Edgar 59, 60
Bauer, Lt Col Joseph, USMC 69
Bauer, Maj Harold, USMC **39**, 76
Brewster F2A-1 8, 11, 13, 15, 58

"Cactus Air Force" 60, 64, 69
Carl, Capt Marion, USMC 16, **17**, 58, 64, **66**, 66, 69, **72**, 74, 76
Chance Vought XF4U-1 Corsair 7, **77**, 77
Cheek, Machinist Tom 58, **59**, 59
Chiyoda (Japanese light carrier) 51
Conger, Lt Jack, USMC 76
Coral Sea, Battle of 38, 39, 56-8, 73-4

Dibb, Ens Robert "Ram" 59-60, 60-1, **62-3**
Doyle, 2Lt Cecil "Danny", USMC 74, 76
drop tanks 22, 22, 61

Eastern Aircraft Division, FM-2 Wildcats 77, **78**
Eastern Solomons, Battle of 40, 64, 65, 74
Endo, PO3/c Masuaki 75
Enterprise, USS (CV-6) **9**, **37**, **38**, 58, 61, **70**, 70
Everton, Capt Loren, USMC 76

Flatley, Lt Cdr James 6, 56, **57**, 57-8, 61, 70, 71, 75
Foss, Capt Joseph, USMC **cover 2**, **29**, **50**, 50, 58, 69, 70, **74**, 74, 75-6, 76
Frank, Richard (historian) 73
Frazer, 2Lt Kenneth, USMC 76
Freeman, 2Lt William, USMC 76
Fuchida, Mitsuo 43
Fukumori, PO3/c Daizo 75

Galer, Maj Robert, USMC 64, 68, 76
Gaylor, Lt Noel **cover 2**
Greenwood, TSgt R W, USMC **7**
Grumman:
    F3F-3 **11**, 11
    F4F-3 Wildcats **cover 9**, 9, 14, **15**, 15, 15-16, 16, **26**, 26-7, 28, 29, **37**, **56**, 56, 58, **72**
    F4F-3A 16, **27**, 27
    F4F-4 Wildcats **5**, 6, 7, **16**, 16, **17**, **28**, 28-9, **29**, **39**, **58**, **66**, 66-7, **68**, **70**, **71**, **72**
        cockpit layout **44**
        vs A6M Zero-Sen 6, 34, 39, 67, 73
    Martlet I (F4F-3) 15, 27
    Martlet III (F4F-3A) 16, 27
    XF4F-1 8, 11
    XF4F-2 8, **12**, 12-13, **13**, 25-6
    XF4F-3 8, **9**, 9, 13-14, **14**, 26
    XF4F-4 9, 16
    XF4F-6 16, 27
    XF6F Hellcat 7, 77, 78
Guadalcanal 6, 39, 40, 50, 52, 60-1, 64, 66, 69-70, 70-1, 73-4
    Henderson Field **5**, **40**, 60, **64**, 64, **65**, **66**, 66, **67**, 71

Habermann, 2Lt Roger, USMC **74**, 76
Hamilton, Mar Gun Henry, USMC 76
Hashiguchi, PO2/c Yoshiro 20, **51**, 51
Hass, Ens Walter 56
Hiryu (Japanese carrier) 39
Horikoshi, Jiro (designer) 18, 19, 20, 22, 23, 30
Hornet, USS (CV-8) 16, **58**, 58, 70

IJN:
    "Decisive Battle" concept 41-2
    Koku Hombu (Aviation Bureau) 18, 19, 20, 22, 32
IJNAF (Imperial Japanese Navy Air Force):
    builds Guadalcanal air base 39
    fighter tactics 49, 52, 68
        shotai formation 49, **52**, 52, **54**, 57
        slow roll 71
    initial Zero-Sen campaign 4-5, 35-6, 51, 52
    Kokutais (air groups), 2nd 39; 3rd 35, 51; Tainan 35, 39, **40**, **61**, 61, 66, **67**, 74, **75**
    manpower philosophy 41-2
    pilot recruitment 42
    pilot training 42-3
Ishikawa, PO3/c Seiji 75

Kaga (Japanese carrier) 39
Kaigun (Navy of the Greater Japanese Empire):
    defense in depth tactics 37, 38
    Operations *MO* and *MI* 38
Kimura, PO3/c Yutaka 75
Kirk, Jr, Lt Kenneth, USMC 71
Kleinman, Lt (jg) John 53
Kobayashi, PO1/c Katsumi 75
Kokubu, PO3/c Takeichi 75
Kumagai, PO3/c Kenichi 75

Lexington, USS (CV-2) 38, 56
Long Island, USS (ACV-1) 61
Lundstrom, John (historian) 41, 60, 73

McCusky, Lt (jg) Scott 76
machine guns:
    0.30in 15, 26
    7.7mm 19, 30-1, 32, **33**, 34, 67, 75
    Browning M2 0.50in 12, 15, 16, 25, 26, 28, **29**, 34, 75
Macomber, Lt (jg) Brainard 59, 60
Marontate, Bill 74
Midway, Battle of **38**, 39, 43, 58-60, **59**, 73-4
Mitsubishi:
    A5M Type 96 8, **18**, 18-19, 22, 32, 51, 56
    A5M4-K Type 96 Trainer 43
    A6M1 (Zuisei-13) 22, 23, 30
    A6M2 Zero-Sen Model 11 9, **23**, 23, **31**, 31
    A6M2 Zero-Sen Model 21 **cover**, 2, 4, 4-5, 6, **8**, 8, 12, **20**, 20, **21**, 23, **24**, 24, 31-2, **32**, **33**, **36**, 39, 56, **64**, **69**, **70**
        cockpit layout 45
        vs F4F Wildcats 6, 34, 39, 67, 73
    A6M3 Zero-Sen Model 32 **6**, **9**, 24, 33, **34**, 39, 61
    A6M5 Zero-Sen Model 52 **78**, 78
    Prototype 12-shi 8, 18, 22, 30
Miya, PO3/c Unichi 75

Nakajima Aircraft Company 24, 32
Nakakariya, PO3/c Kunimori 23
Nakano, PO2/c Shin 75
Narr, Lt Joseph, USMC 76
Nishizawa, PO1/c Hiroyoshi 75

O'Hare, Lt Butch 70
Ohashi, PO3/c Yoshizo 75
Okumiya, Masatake 43
Ota, PO2/c Toshio 75

Pearl Harbor 6, **22**, 36
Percy, Lt James, USMC 76
Peterson, Ens Dale 2
Pierce, Capt Francis, USMC 76
Pond, 2Lt Kenneth 76

Rabaul, New Britain 37, 39, **40**, 40, 60-1, **61**, 64, **65**, 66, **75**

radio communications 32, 52, 55, 59, 68
Ranger, USS (CV-4) 15
Register, Ens Francis 64, 76
Rhodes, Radio Technician Thomas **64**
Rowell, Ens Richard 2
Royal Australian Navy Coastwatchers 61, 64
Ruddell, Roy **74**
Ryūjō (Japanese light carrier) 64

Sakai, PO1/c Saburo, *Samurai!* 43, 67, **68**, **75**
Santa Cruz, Battle of 40, 65, **70**, 70, **71**, 74
Saratoga, USS (CV-3) 61, 64
Sasai, Lt (jg) Junichi 66, **67**
Sawruk, James (historian) 73
self-sealing fuel tanks 15, 20, 27, 29, 39, 74, 75
Sheedy, Ens Daniel 58
Shima, Kasuzo (test pilot) 22
Shindo, Lt Saburo 22
Shingo, Lt Hideki 71
Shōhō (Japanese light carrier) 38, 56
Shōkaku (Japanese carrier) **24**, 38, 51, 56, 66, **71**
Simpler, Lt Cdr Leroy 64
Smith, Maj John L, USMC 64, 66, **67**, 68, 74, 75, 76
Soryu (Japanese carrier) 39
Southerland, Lt J J **68**
Stearman N25 Primary Trainer **46**
Suzuki, Lt Minoru 23

Thach, Lt Cdr John "Jimmy" **1**, 6, **53**, 54-6, 58-60, **59**, 60-1, **62-3**, 75

USMC (US Marine Corps):
    1st Marine Division 40
    1st MAW (Marine Air Wing) 6, **7**, 36, **39**, 60, 61, 70, 73
    fighter squadrons VMF-121 69, 71, **74**, 76; VMF-124 **77**; VMF-212 69, 71, 76; VMF-221 (on Midway); VMF-223 61, 64, 66-7, 68, 69, 76; VMF-224 64, 66-7, 68, 69, 76
    pilot training 46-7, **47**
USN:
    Advanced Carrier Training Groups 48, 50
    aerial gunnery 48, 48, **72**
    Bureau of Aeronautics 10-11
    December 1941 establishment 36
    fighter squadrons, VF-2 2, 53, 56-7; VF-3 **1**, **53**, 54, 58, **59**, 60, 76; VF-4 **15**, 15; VF-5 **53**, 53, 61, 64, 68-9, 76; VF-6 58, 61, **64**, 64, 76; VF-7 **26**; VF-8 **58**, 58; VF-10 58, **70**, 70, 71; VF-42 **26**, 56-7, 76; VF-71 61
    fighter tactics:
        against Type 1 (Mitsubishi G4M) bombers 66-7
        head on attacks 69-70
        "Hints to Navy VF Pilots" 57-8, 69, 75
        "Thach Weave" 6, 54-6, **55**, 59-60, 60-1, **62-3**, 70, 75
        two-plane formation 53
    manpower philosophy 41
    Pacific Fleet, lightning raids 37
    pilot recruitment 46
    pilot training **47**, 47-8, 76
    Two-Ocean Navy Act 36, 48

Wasp, USS (CV-7) 15, 1661

Yamamoto, Seaman 1/c Kenichiro 75
Yokosuka, K5Y1/2 Type 93 Intermediate Trainer 42, 42
Yonekawa, Seaman 1/c Masayoshi 75
Yorktown, USS (CV-5) **26**, 39, 56, 58, 60
Yost, Maj Donald, USMC 71, 76

Zuikaku (Japanese carrier) 38, 56, 66